The F

in my

Bouquet

Susie Williams

Susie Williams

ISBN: 1502724073
ISBN-13: 978-1502724076

The Flowers in my Bouquet

First published as a Kindle book, September 2014

First Printed by Create Space, November 2014

Also by Susie Williams

From Goats to a Garden, first published June 2013

Kindle Edition ASIN B00DP6P48O

Paperback Edition ISBN 978-149369444O

Both available from Amazon and other book stores

Front cover photo

Evan and Susannah Voyce with their children
Sidney, Florry and Walter

CONTENTS

List of Illustrations

Acknowledgements

I am indebted to my cousins Richard Voice and William Clark for providing invaluable family information and photographs.

Hereford Archives for assistance in researching the Saint family.

Hereford Library Archives for facilitating access to historic newspaper items from The Hereford Times.

Most of all I am grateful to my husband for editing this book.

Additional information and all the photographs in full colour can be found on the author's website,

www.susiewilliams.coffeecup.com

where the family trees are also reproduced.

Introduction

Some years ago I decided to research my family history. I was fascinated with the interaction of historical events with the lives of my family members, with the impact on them of disease, social conditions and war. In this book I have attempted to weave a story around my ancestors. Most of the events related here are historically accurate, and the principal characters were real people; this is the story of what happened to them from 1760 onwards. I have invented some supporting characters. As the story unfolds the strands draw together, to become my family in Birmingham.

Chapter One

Who do I think I am?

I am standing by the telephone, listening to the ringing tone. I have dialled the number carefully, apprehensively. When the phone is answered - if the phone is answered - I shall be speaking to the half-sister I have never spoken to before; the half-sister I have never met.

I can't believe this is actually happening. Ever since I was a child I had known there was a half-sister somewhere, but that I should ever be able to speak to her or to meet her was way beyond probability, or so I thought.

I had been adopted when I was a few weeks old and my adoptive parents were very open about the facts of my adoption. They told me that I was born as a result of a love affair between my widowed mother and a married man during the Second World War and they told me that my mother had a daughter from her marriage.

I was always curious about my natural family but I had a very good home and out of loyalty to the parents who had brought me up I did nothing to try to trace my mother. I did however obtain my original birth certificate when I was nearly fifty. So there was my mother's name, Hetty, with her married name and what was relevant to me, her maiden name, Voyce. As I was an illegitimate baby there was, of course, no entry under the name of father.

Ten years or so went by and from time to time I wondered

if my mother was still alive and how one went about trying to trace a mother who possibly did not want to be traced. I had also been told that my adoptive mother and my natural mother were a very similar age. As my adoptive mother, born in 1903 had died by then, I knew it was quite possible that my natural mother had also died. But still I was curious to know more about her.

And then the wonders of the internet opened up and I discovered that there was easy access to birth, marriage and death records and so the search began.

I started by trying to trace my mother's marriage. Assuming she was married when she was in her twenties, armed with her maiden name and her married name I started looking in the 1920s and found her marriage in 1926. I sent for her marriage certificate and when it arrived I found out that she was born in 1904 and I also found that her father was called Evan Charles Voyce and that he had been a jeweller.

The next thing to discover was her exact date of birth. As she had been born in January 1904 I soon found her record and sent off for her birth certificate. She had been born on 17th January. This gave me the name of her mother, Susannah, whose maiden name was Hall. And so the search for my ancestors was well under way and I was so excited to be able to start to build up my family tree.

It was 2004 when I was making these discoveries so unless Hetty was very long lived, it was unlikely that I would find her still alive. Finding her death took quite a while but eventually I discovered that she had died on the 21st March 1981. It was quite a coincidence that my adoptive mother had died in October the same year.

I sent for her death certificate and this is when my search began to get even more interesting for I discovered that it was Hetty's daughter who had been present at her death and whose signature was there on the death certificate.

So the mysterious half-sister now had a name, and furthermore her address in a pleasant area in the Midlands was also on the certificate. It occurred to me that she could very possibly still be alive. The electoral roll for that area was consulted and it seemed that the search was already at an end when I discovered that she no longer lived at the address on Hetty's death certificate. However my husband, who was helping me with this search, saw her name in the list of addresses further down the same road. At last there she was and it seemed that she was still alive.

That was amazing. To think that I had spent my entire life not knowing anyone who was related to me except my two sons and now here was a half-sister. This was getting very exciting.

But a big quandary presented itself. Did she know anything about me? Did she know that her mother had given birth to an illegitimate baby or had Hetty gone away and had her baby secretly? I wanted to contact her but I spent a long time wondering if it was the right thing to do.

Eventually I wrote to her including a copy of my birth certificate to prove who I was. Now the ball was in her court. Would she even reply I wondered?

I have to use the word 'amazing' again because yes, she did

reply and it was by return of post. She seemed to be as excited as I was that I had contacted her and asked me to phone her as soon as possible.

Hence, there I was on that early March day, waiting for her to answer the phone and to set in motion a chain of events that has changed my life.

And of course she did answer the phone and there was great excitement shown by both of us.

"Did you know about me?" I asked her.

"Oh yes," she said, "I held you when you were just a few hours old." Well that was a bit tear jerking!

She told me that despite my birth being nearly sixty-two years ago she had never forgotten me and always particularly remembered me on my birthday in August.

We knew we wanted to meet so a few weeks later my husband and I made the journey north from where we lived in the south of England. It was so exciting but I was also apprehensive. Would we like each other? What would she look like?

I need have had no worries. Immediately we took to each other and spent a lovely and happy few hours together. She was a very similar height to me and had a very warm personality. It may seem weird but we also found out that we had both inherited Hetty's bunions which I believe are carried down the female line.

What was particularly interesting was that she was able to tell me my father's name. She well remembered the love affair between him and our mother. She was still a school girl at the time and told me how she would come home from school and he would be there and, feeling unwanted and in the way, she used to take the dog out for a walk.

By now I had begun to build up my family tree and was delighted that she was able to lend me some family photos which we were able to copy before returning them to her. It was so interesting to see a picture of my mother and my grandparents and their other children. Now I had a family. And here is that word again. It truly was 'amazing'.

I said to her, "I'm wondering if our grandfather's name, Evan, being a Welsh name means we have Welsh blood in us?"

"Oh yes," she said, "there was talk of a Welsh grandmother living next door."

In recent years the television programme 'Who Do You Think You Are?' has been very popular. Back then in 2004, I was able to start finding out who I was and this is what this book is about.

Part of the Watkin family from Montgomeryshire is in me as is part of the Howells family from the Long Mynd in Shropshire and the Saints from Hereford whose ancestors had come across the sea from America. Part of the Voyce family from Warwickshire is in me; the family that variously spelled their name as Voice, Voyce, Vise, Vice and Voce.

I was able to place these people in history; there among the Drovers who brought cattle from Wales through

Shropshire to England; and the Watkin family, millers in Kerry in Wales; William Saint, the shoemaker in Hereford; Mary Saint who grew up in Hereford Workhouse, and her marriage to William Hall, the rogue policeman born in Northamptonshire; and also the agricultural labourers from what was then the tiny village of Castle Bromwich in Warwickshire.

I was able to trace how all these family lines converged on the growing town of Birmingham in the time of Queen Victoria and what happened to them next.

William and Mary Hall's daughter Susannah, my grandmother, is a major character in this story which charts her years as a teacher followed by her time as a housemaid then her marriage to Evan Voyce and the ups and downs of her child bearing years. There are her aspirations for her second son Walter which helped her to overcome the tragedy of Evan's untimely death. I have written about the impact of the Boer War and the tragedies of the First World War which left a great mark on the Voyce/Voice family.

For the most part it is historically accurate although I have used my imagination to fill in the gaps in what I hope is a realistic way. The completely fictional characters are William Williams, The Prossers in Hereford, Mrs Parker, Mr Davenport, the Robertson family and their household, Florence Smith and the Italian photographer. They are entirely the work of my imagination.

That visit to my half-sister was not the only one. Throughout the year we kept in touch with many letters and telephone calls and in August on my birthday we went to see her again. She had a bottle of champagne ready to celebrate the occasion and gave to me a card. 'To my dear Sister' it said.

Well just think of that! In all my years of being an only child here was I at sixty-two with a sister. Yes, again it was 'amazing'.

She stood up and went to fetch a wooden box saying there were some things in it that she would like me to have. We sat next to each other on her sofa while she lifted the lid and the layers of family history revealed themselves.

Here was a photo of our mother, Hetty aged about thirty-five, standing next to lovely, dependable Florry; here a later photo of Hetty, smiling coquettishly into the camera; here my grandfather Evan and my grandmother Susannah with their children, Sidney, Florry, dear blonde haired Walter and chubby Hetty sitting on Susannah's lap; here is Evan, already looking gaunt, holding on to the back of the chair for support. Susannah with a worried looking frown is sitting on the chair, her lips primly pinched together.

Then out of the Box came a collection of birth, marriage and death certificates to which, as time went by, I added many more.

She also gave me the locket containing the picture of Walter in uniform that Susannah had worn around her neck.

Near the bottom of the box, hidden away for many years is the wedding photograph from 1890, a symbol of hope for a new life, a moment frozen in time signifying a new start, with Evan, tall and upright, proud of his new status as a married man, seated with one hand on a cane, smart in his new suit, moustache carefully waxed. Susannah, unsmiling, standing at his side, slightly to the back showing respect for her new husband, her hand on the back of his chair signifying her connection to him or was it subservience?

Her dress is cinched in tightly at the waist, her hair piled high on her head, her eyes staring straight at the camera.

Who were the other people in the picture?

Susannah's mother Mary is there. Surely she is hoping and praying that Susannah has found a good man in Evan and that their union will be long and happy with a marriage enriched by children.

A shadowy figure in the background is William, Susannah's father. Although I didn't know it at the time when I was with my sister, later on as I found out more about the family I realised that well might he hang his head in shame. He was father to Susannah and her siblings but also father of at least one child born out of wedlock, maybe more.

Who is that other woman? The one with round cheeks and lips upturned at the corners waiting to give a friendly smile to her new daughter in law? She must be Sarah, the Welsh mother of Evan. Later I discovered that as a girl she came all the way from Wales to find work in Birmingham where she fell in love with Evan's father Charley who only just got her to the altar before Evan was born.

And there is Charley with his weather beaten face and twinkly eyes.

Down at the bottom of the box are a few dried petals and a neatly folded length of faded blue ribbon. As I lifted up the petals and let them drift down from my fingers, my romantic mind told me these were the remnants of Susannah's wedding bouquet, now crumbled to dust; faded and gone just as the people here have also all passed away.

Before I continue with the story of my ancestors I must say that sadly that visit on my birthday was the last time I saw my dear half-sister for, although we continued to keep in touch, during the following winter she became ill and died in February 2005. How I missed her and do to this day but meeting her changed my life and helped me to discover who I really am.

And this is where the story that is fiction wrapped around fact begins; first we go right back to Ann Howells, born in 1769 at a farm on the Long Mynd in Shropshire, who had two illegitimate children whose baptisms, like hers, are recorded in the records of the church of St John the Baptist at Myndtown, Shropshire.

Chapter Two

On the Drovers' Trail

It is 1807. A woman and her young daughter are walking slowly along the crest of the hill on the old drovers' road on the Long Mynd. They smile at each other. Up here the air is pure and the larks rise singing into the cloudless sky. In the blue distance are the mountains of Wales. On a warm, spring day like this it is as near to heaven as you can get.

"Come along, Sarah," Ann says holding out her hand, "it's time to go back and get your Grandfather's tea ready." With one last look at the distant hills they turn down the track that leads to the farm nestled into the hillside below them.

****

Ann Howells was born at Myndtown in Shropshire in 1769. She was the daughter of Thomas Howells and his wife Jane. Thomas was a sheep farmer on the Welsh Borders and they lived in the tiny hamlet of Myndtown.

When Ann was a girl, she loved to climb up the Long Mynd on the tracks through the bracken and gorse with her long hair flowing out behind her and running, full of life and vigour, chasing her twin sister Jane with younger sister Martha trying to catch up with them.

From the top of the hills there were far distant views with Clee Hill and the smoke of Coalbrookdale in one direction and the other way back towards Wales with pure air and the high mountains.

In the spring the snow lingered late in the gullies and the melt-water rushed down the hillsides in torrents. In early summer the air was fresh and clean. Fluffy white clouds scudded overhead and larks rose from the short sheep-cropped turf where the heather shoots were showing spiky green buds.

At the foot of the hills there was the tiny white chapel with its rough stone font where all the children had been baptised. Ann, with her brother Thomas and her sisters would sit there on Sundays on the hard, varnished pews in their starched Sunday best, gazing at the stained glass window behind the small altar, trying to listen to a lengthy sermon while their thoughts were on the delicious dinner that would be served up when they got home.

1. The Church at Myndtown

As Ann grew into young womanhood her love of life did

not diminish. She helped to herd the sheep and bring them down from the hillside at shearing time. She rolled the fleeces, some for sale and some for spinning and weaving at home. She learned to card and then spin the wool, first on a drop spindle and later on a spinning wheel; to use vegetable dyes to colour the wool and finally to knit or weave it into clothes to be worn by the family and colourful shawls and blankets to keep them warm in the long winters.

She and her sisters had to learn about cheese and butter making and how to make bread and all the different preserves that would keep them going through the winter. There were hams and flitches of bacon to salt down and sausages to make. It was a busy life enlivened by market days in Bishop's Castle where the farm produce like eggs, butter and cheese were sold and gossip and news were exchanged.

Each year when the winter was over there was the excitement of the drovers coming with huge herds of black cattle on their way to England. Blacksmiths had fitted the cattle with iron shoes to protect their feet during the long journey and then on they went to be fattened up for the markets in London. One of the men would come along a day or so beforehand and negotiate with Thomas for the animals to graze for a few days in one of his lowland pastures, to rest before they continued their journey.

The drovers would sleep in a barn and meals would be provided for them in the house. It was a small but useful source of extra income for Ann's father. Then after three or four days when the animals and men were rested, off they would go again, up and over the Long Mynd on the ancient drove roads and on their way to pastures in Kent and Sussex, avoiding the turnpike roads whenever possible to save money.

When Ann was a girl the cattle walked all the way from Wales to London but much later when the railways came they were herded into cattle trucks at Shrewsbury and then went by train for the rest of their journey.

Season followed season and the pattern of life was unchanging. Ann grew to womanhood and longed to get married, to have a family and to move away from her childhood home to a home of her own. Her mother had become ill and died when she was twenty and as her sisters one by one had married and moved to their own homes Ann had taken responsibility for all the domestic chores of the household.

But the years went on and by the time she was in her mid-twenties she felt that life was passing her by. Each year when the drovers came she would hear stories of life beyond her quiet valley and would be filled with longing to go over the hills with them, to meet people and to see a different kind of life.

In 1796 she thought that at last her wishes might come true. When the drovers came that year in the spring her father was away in Ludlow where he had gone to see an elderly relation, so it was Ann who dealt with the drover who came in advance of the others to settle a price for the grazing for three days and to see which field the animals would go in. He introduced himself, "William Williams is my name ma'am."

He was a tall, weather beaten Welshman, aged about thirty, wearing a rough tweed coat and battered hat and Ann found herself attracted to him in no small way. As it was raining she asked him into the farmhouse kitchen. He tied his horse up in the yard and, removing his hat before ducking his head beneath the low lintel, he entered the house.

It was a chilly spring day and the aromatic smell of wood smoke from the fire in the range pervaded the air. He pulled out a chair and sat at the well-scrubbed table while she fetched him cider, bread and cheese. While she was cutting the bread and fetching cheese from the dairy at the back of the house he gazed around.

There were hams and fat sausages hanging in the inglenook, a basket of new laid eggs was waiting to be checked over and in a bowl near the fire dough for bread making had been set to rise. A rag rug was spread on the stone flagged floor in front of the range and a cat dozed lazily on a chair in the corner next to a spinning wheel. Gazing wistfully on the homely scene he said, "Good place you've got here missus, only one thing missing."

"Oh yes, what's that then?" Ann asked as she turned towards him.

"Well I don't hear any children running around laughing."

"That's because there aren't any. My sisters have married and moved away and my brother is courting; but he won't be tying the knot for some time to come."

"And you?"

"Well you're the cheeky one aren't you, with all your questions. But since you're asking I'm just stuck here doing the chores as I always have done day by day. Romance has passed me by. And in any case who is there to look after my Pa but me?" She sighed and pursed her lips.

"I envy you your life here. You're settled and have a roof over your head and a fire to sit by out of the wind and the rain. I am always on the road in all weathers. Not only do we have the cattle to cope with and find pasturage for but also we carry letters and money across the country. Sometimes it's quite hefty sums of money we carry for traders and sometimes we get attacked and robbed, even on occasion a drover gets killed. What wouldn't I give to have a lovely wife like you to come home to? No missus, it's you who are to be envied."

Ann was silent for a few minutes while the impact of William's words sank in.

"William you make me see my situation in a different way. You're right I do have a good home and I am thankful for that but what I don't have is a strong man to care for me and give me children."

And with that, as a tear trickled slowly down her cheek, she turned away and poured him some cider from a stone jug that stood on the dresser. Wiping the tear away with the back of her hand she put his drink on the table and their eyes met and they held each other's gaze for a few seconds.

It could have been at that moment that the bond between them that was to have such an impact on her life was made.

A short time later, when they had discussed which field was to be used for the cattle the next day, they went outside and Ann pointed out the barn where the men could sleep on straw filled sacks. The rain had stopped and the sun shone fitfully between the showers. On the Long Mynd a rainbow arched over the fresh new green on the trees above the farm where the drovers track led up the hill.

"Mam used to say a rainbow is a good omen, a sign of good luck." Ann said, "Isn't it beautiful?"

William looked at her and said with a smile, "It's not the only thing round here that's beautiful."

Ann blushed and laughed as she realised he was talking about her. He drew a finger slowly down her soft cheek and the back of her neck tingled with pleasure. "Ann, you're a lovely lady."

He reluctantly drew away from her, raised his hand in farewell, mounted his horse and rode back towards Bishop's Castle and the herd of cattle slowly making their way towards Myndtown across the moors from the other side of Kerry. But his thoughts were not on the cattle but on the woman he had left behind him and whom he would see again in a few short hours.

Thomas returned next day, tired after his journey on horseback and Ann was able to tell him that the drovers were on their way and would be arriving soon. "I hope you sorted out the price for the grazing," Thomas said gruffly,

"I could do with some extra money just now.

"Yes, it's all arranged and space for them to sleep in the barn. And they'll eat in here and pay for that too."

"You've done well lass."

Later that afternoon, long before they could be seen, the barking dogs, the whistled signals and shouts of the drovers and the bellowing of cattle could be heard coming through the woods along the valley. William came ahead on his horse but the three other men were on foot. The farm dogs were shut in a barn to avoid fights breaking out with the strangers' dogs. The dust rose as the black cattle came into the yard and were herded into the field that William pointed out. The men were tired and hungry and were glad to be shown to the barn where they were to sleep and even more pleased to be told that a meal would be ready for them at the farmhouse in half an hour.

Ann came out in her apron to check that all the arrangements she had made were satisfactory. "William, is everything all right?" she called out.

He came over to her. "Here is my beautiful lady again," he said with a smile and a twinkle in his brown eyes. Ann felt her heartbeat quicken and blushing with pleasure, she looked up at him. "Yes it is," he replied, "and we're all glad to be here. The cattle and men have walked over twenty miles today from Kerry and they're all exhausted. It's a high track over moors with wonderful views but we have to be very vigilant that the cattle don't wander off. We'll be glad to rest here for a few days before we set off again and press on towards Hereford and into England."

Ann recovered her composure. "I must hurry to complete the meal preparations. Come in when you're ready. It's good to have you here again."

She bustled off to get bread out of the oven and to stir the enormous pot of stew that bubbled on the range. She fetched the spoons out of the drawer in the dresser and placed them and two large crockery jugs of cider on the table near a large pat of freshly made butter. There was plum jam in an earthenware dish and a sharp knife to cut the bread with. Bowls were warming near the range. Just as William and the men crowded through the door she was standing back looking at the spread on the table to make sure everything they needed was there.

The men didn't have much to say and apart from a brief "Good evening missus," they pulled out their chairs and sat at the table. Ann ladled the stew into the bowls and the men set to, dipping the hunks of bread into the savoury gravy and shovelling spoonfuls of food into their mouths.

"Ann, this is good," William complemented her before tucking in with great relish. As the bowls became empty Ann refilled them and cut more bread. When the stew was finished butter and jam were spread on the bread and tankards were replenished with the good farm cider.

Before darkness fell the men trooped off to the barn leaving William in the warm kitchen with Ann. She lit a tallow candle and carefully placed it in its stand on the windowsill where it would guide her father into the house when he came back from checking the sheep. The in-lamb ewes had been brought down from the hill to be nearer to the farm because it was lambing time now and it was important to keep an eye on them and to spot any ewes that were likely to give birth soon. She pulled up a chair and sat at the table opposite William.

"Ann I don't know why there isn't a trail of handsome swains queuing up at the door to marry you. You're a wonderful cook and, as we all know, the way to a man's heart is through his stomach."

As she rested her hands on the table he reached out and put his hands over hers. He was just about to speak again when a loud clumping of boots was heard coming up the path and her father, Thomas, came into the room. William stood up, his chair scraping noisily over the flagstones.

"My, there's a nip in the air outside tonight," Thomas said rubbing his hands together in front of the fire to get some warmth back in them. As Ann put a bowl of steaming stew and a hunk of bread on the table for him he turned to William.

"Is everything out there to your liking young man? Cattle well pastured, men satisfied with their sleeping quarters and food arrangements?"

"Yes sir and we're very glad to be here. The last few days have been tough coming over the mountains. The easier part lies ahead passing over the Herefordshire hills and through the lowlands."

After William had gone off to the barn with the other men for the night Thomas finished his meal and sat by the fire deep in thought while Ann washed the dishes. When she had finished she picked up her knitting and came to sit by him. He took his pipe out of his mouth, tapped it on the hearth and laid it down next to the range.

"Ann, my dear I've been thinking. Seeing you with a big strong fellow like that I realise that you're missing out on having a man of your own. Your mother and I had many happy years together. Times were often hard but we had a roof over our heads, a fire to sit by and always food of some sort on the table. William seems to be a good fellow from what I hear so if you want to give him some encouragement you can do it with my blessing. If you find he feels the same way well and good."

He picked up his pipe again and pressed some tobacco down into the bowl. Lifting up a taper from near the fire, he held it to the flames until it was alight and then held it to his pipe. When that was issuing clouds of smoke he blew out the taper and settled down to puff away at the pipe but it seemed he had not yet finished his discourse to Ann.

"I'm jumping the gun a bit here but, should it get as far as marriage, being the wife of a drover might be hard but who's to say he won't settle down in a year or so anyway and what better place to settle down than here? Mind you I don't know how I'd manage without you here if he wanted to take you away. You're such a good daughter to me, but then young Thomas is courting a nice girl and he'll be taking over the farm from me in a few years so his wife will have to run this place."

Ann was amazed that her father had been so forthright but it certainly made her think that as she liked William anyway and time was short she'd better take her father's advice and set about doing some encouraging as soon as possible.

She was up before dawn milking the house cow and when that was finished she carried the brimming pail of milk over to the kitchen. Some of the milk was poured into a small churn and put into the north-facing dairy to keep cool. That would provide milk for the house during the day. The rest she placed in pancheons on the wide slate shelves in the dairy to let the cream settle and rise to the top of the milk. Later in the day she would use a skimmer to carefully remove it and put some of it in the newly acquired barrel churn. She would collect the cream from two or three days' milk before she started to churn it. It was a laborious job turning the handle constantly until she could hear a regular thud; then she knew the butter had come. Taking the golden lump of butter out of the churn she would put it on the cool slate slab and using a pat in each hand she would methodically pat and turn the lump of butter thus squeezing the remaining buttermilk out of it. The buttermilk from the churn would be tipped into a pail and would eventually be used for cooking or would go to feed the pigs.

But this morning there was breakfast to be made for hungry men. Lifting down a flitch of bacon from the inglenook she cut off thick slices and placed them in a large frying pan on the range where they sizzled and started to give off a mouth-watering aroma. She could hear the men talking in the yard and hurriedly laid the table and got a loaf of bread out of the crock.

As they came through the door she started to break eggs into another pan and was soon serving up a hearty breakfast to them. Thomas came in and joined them and the conversation turned to talk of moving livestock, the weather and the price of cattle.

Ann was too busy replenishing the plates to catch William's eye until breakfast was over. Her father quickly went out to the field where lambing was in full progress and suddenly they were alone again. She was wiping crumbs from the table when he came and stood by her.

"Ann there isn't much time as we'll be off in a day or two but I've seen enough of you to know that already I love you. Will you be my girl and wait for me when I come this way again? I'm sure we are meant for each other."

She looked up at him, her heart beating more quickly,

"I think I've been waiting all my life for you William and as long as you come as often as you can I shall be happy."

They stepped towards each other; eagerly she put her arms round his neck and drew his head down to her lips. He enfolded her in his arms and they stood entwined, lost to the world in an everlasting kiss, their young bodies pressed closely together. When eventually they drew apart it was not because their passion was abating but because it was galloping too quickly away with them.

With her arm still on his shoulder she asked,

"Will you be the strong man I have been waiting for to give me babies William?"

"Ann, my love, yes just as soon as you wish."

The morning hours were moving on rapidly and there were chores that had to be done. Yesterday's April showers had turned to warm sunshine and the breeze briskly flapped the sheets that Ann had hung on the line to dry. Picking up the basket of dry washing later in the morning Ann turned and looked up at the hills and the drove road winding its way upward. A dreadful pang filled her heart as she realised William would soon be gone. Her body yearned for him; she realised she could not let him go without them fulfilling their love for each other.

The opportunity came that afternoon when he took her hand, smiled invitingly at her and led her up the hill and out onto the moor. In sheltered places the primroses were flowering, the windflowers nodded in the breeze and the new bright fronds of bracken uncurled in the warm sunshine.

They found a patch of dry heather sheltered by a group of gorse bushes where William spread his coat and pulled her down to lie beside him. There was no time for lengthy preliminaries to their lovemaking. Their need for each other was so urgent. Passionate kisses were followed by William's caresses that moved from her open bodice and full breasts down her body. He pulled off his breeches, lifted her skirt and pushed her legs apart. His exploring hands moved up her smooth thighs and reached the dampness of their goal.

"Ann, my love," he groaned as he thrust into her, sealing her brief cry of pain with his lips. They moved together and rejoiced in each other's rising passion. At last it was done and they lay breathlessly side-by-side.

"You were a virgin, I see. Next time there will be no pain."

"Next time it will be even better then," she replied.

Sometime later they went back down the hill where from his vantage spot in the sheep field Thomas saw them coming. A smile crossed his face, "My daughter has found herself a man," he thought to himself, "and is no longer as she was. The bird has been caught and put in the cage."

The rain returned again that evening and the gentle breeze of the morning turned into a gale that rattled the windowpanes. Tomorrow the drovers would be on their way again. William would be gone. As Ann sat at the table with him she knew it would be weeks until she saw him again. From his corner by the fire Thomas looked across at them and his heart melted. He knew his daughter had met her soul mate and that they should have this last night together.

"Young William, you'd better sleep in the house tonight. Ann will find you a bed. It's rough out there. You need your sleep before you go on your way." His daughter looked at him gratefully and William smiled.

"Thanks Pa," she said giving him a hug but it wasn't sleep that either she or William had in mind.

That night their love making, all of it, proceeded at a slower pace. The kisses, the caresses and finally the coming together were given time and fully savoured.

Ann woke before dawn and gazed lovingly at William, still asleep. Reluctantly she dressed and picking up her shoes tiptoed down the wooden staircase to prepare a good breakfast to set the drovers up for the day ahead. Shortly after daybreak the cattle were in the yard, the dogs circling round them excitedly and the men were ready to be off. William saddled up his horse and leaving it tied to the fence came into the kitchen where Ann was dejectedly clearing the breakfast plates away. As he held her for one last time she said, "Come back to me William, as soon as you can." He clasped her tightly, kissed her and replied,

"Just as soon as I can, my love." And with that he jammed his hat on his head, mounted his horse and rode away leading the herd up the hill.

Stepping out into the yard with the hens clucking round her feet Ann sadly watched as the cattle, men and dogs wound their way up the slopes of the Long Mynd on the old drovers road. Finally, silhouetted against the skyline William turned and waved to her down in the valley and then he was gone.

Life on the farm resumed its usual pattern. Lambing drew to a close and when the days were warmer the sheep were sheared and Ann selected the fleeces she wanted for spinning. Calves were born and there was an abundance of milk, which heralded cheese-making time. The rich milk of summer was poured into pancheons, rennet was added and the curds were left to form. Later they were cut and the whey was drained away. Ann mixed salt with the crumbly curds and packed them into slatted moulds. These were put on the dairy shelf to drain. After a while the cheeses were firm enough to be removed from the moulds and salt was rubbed into them. A good crust of greenish-grey mould developed and the cheeses were carefully stored on the dairy shelves in the cool where they were turned and matured over the coming months.

As high summer came Ann began to look up onto the hill hoping that one day she would again see William although it was still too soon to tell him what she was suspecting.

One very hot day at the end of June the farm dogs started barking and she heard horses clattering into the yard. With her hopes building she rushed out and to her great joy there he was with just two horses. He hurriedly dismounted and looping the reins over a gatepost he ran across the yard, drew her to him and hugged her.

"Ann, my love, here I am again and you look just as lovely as ever."

"William I've been looking out for you for a while and now here you are at last. It's so good to see you."

Their lips met and time stood still until a few minutes later he released her.

"Just me and no cattle or men this time but I'm carrying money and important messages so I can only stop for one night and then I must be on my way again. With these two horses I can travel much faster, so less opportunity for ne'er-do-wells to wonder if I'm worth robbing, which I'm afraid I am."

"We must make the most of our one night then mustn't we?" She said with a mischievous look in her eyes. Taking down his saddlebags William said, "I need to find a secure place for these."

"We'll put them under my bed," Ann said, "Then you'll be close to them during the night."

"I hope I'll be close to you too."

"Oh there's no doubt about that." She said with a laugh.

The horses were watered, rubbed down and turned out to pasture and Ann went in to prepare a meal. Thomas had seen William arrive and when the two men had chatted for a while they went indoors where another of Ann's delicious meals awaited them.

Afterwards, arm in arm, Ann and William went out into the farmyard. Thomas smiled to himself as he watched them go. Everything was going according to plan, although somewhat unconventionally but he didn't mind as long as Ann was happy.

The swallows were swooping low over the duck pond catching flies for their hungry nestlings. Open beaks poked out of their mud nests, hanging so precariously under the eaves of the old farmhouse.

"Some of them look as if they're just about to fall out of the nest. They'll be flying soon," Ann said.

"I'll be flying soon as well," William replied, "Over the hills and far away. Come to bed. I need you." So they went in.

Thomas understood their hunger for each other and making excuses about wanting an early night, as it was haymaking on the morrow, he went to his bed.

William and Ann followed him up the narrow wooden stairs soon afterwards. Ann pulled back the crisp white sheets and counterpane as William gently closed the door and checked that his saddlebags were safe. A gentle breeze wafted the curtains to and fro as he drew Ann to him and slipped her dress off her shoulders. As his hands moved over her body she sighed with pleasure and her dress slipped to the floor. His kisses moved from her lips, to her neck and to her breasts. He lifted her up effortlessly and laid her on the bed. He removed his shirt and his breeches and lay by her side. His hands moved downwards, over her belly and onto her legs. His breath came more quickly and his kisses became more passionate. With one hand Ann started to draw him to her and as he raised his body to cover hers she took him with her other hand and guided him into the special place where he wanted so much to be.

Next morning he was off early with his valuable packages. This time, unencumbered by cattle, he would travel quickly and in two days would be back in North Wales. He had told her that in about four weeks he would be back with another drove of cattle having collected them at markets on his way back through the mountains and valleys of Wales. Ann hoped that by that time she would have something definite to tell him.

Following the same pattern as before when the next drove was ten miles or so away William came ahead to give warning of their arrival. Again the men slept in the barn, the cattle were in the field near the church and Ann prepared a filling meal for them all.

By now it was established that William would sleep in Ann's bed. As she lit the candle downstairs and carried it up to the bedroom she was a little apprehensive of what she had to tell him but waited until the bedroom door was closed to give him her news. She put the candle on the washstand while William climbed into bed and held out his hands for her to join him. But she sat on the edge of the bed and anxiously looked at him.

"William I have something to tell you," she began, "I am expecting a baby."

She was startled when he jumped up and stood looking out of the window into the twilight.

"Just give me a few moments to get used to this idea and then we can talk about what we are going to do. You know being the wife of a drover is hard; you get left alone for weeks on end. I would marry you but to take you away from here to live among strangers and then to leave you for long periods doesn't seem right to me." He returned to bed and drew her down to lie with him.

"I agree but there is another way. My father hopes I will stay here with him and that you will give up droving, live here and help run the farm. He doesn't have a lot of faith in Thomas's abilities I'm afraid."

"Ann, I can't do that, at least not yet. Maybe in the future it will work out that way but not yet. I'm earning good money and I can't give that up. Why don't we go on as we are with me coming as often as I can and maybe staying a bit longer each time and see how things work out? And talking of staying longer there's not much time now so blow out that candle and come and lie with me."

So that is what happened and Ann had to make do with a compromise and Thomas had to come to terms with the fact that his plans were not going totally in the way he had hoped they would.

By the time William came that way again it was harvest time and quite obvious that Ann was with child. Their love making now included special kisses for the unborn child within her belly. As he had promised he stayed a few days longer but eventually he had to leave. Telling Ann that with winter coming he would not be that way until the spring made them both realise that by the time he came again their baby would have been born.

And that was the way it turned out.

As autumn moved into winter Ann made jams and preserves and stored them in neat stone jars on the dairy shelves. During the long dark evenings she knitted shawls and made clothes for the baby. Christmas was approaching and the little church was decorated with holly and ivy. The house was full, as some of her sisters had returned with their husbands and children. A goose was killed and stuffed and the spicy smells of Christmas filled the kitchen. The sisters talked over old times while they all helped with the chores. From one or two of them who had not seen her for several months or had not heard her news there were some raised eyebrows when they saw how obviously pregnant she was but a baby born out of wedlock was not that unusual and it would be good to know that there was a child on the farm again.

On Christmas Eve the bird was put to cook overnight in the slow oven on one side of the range and the air began to be filled with the aroma of good things to come.

In the night Ann felt her labour pains starting. For a first baby it was a relatively easy birth and it was good to have her sisters there to be with her during her confinement.

While the rest of the family went to church in the morning she held her baby daughter to her breast and longed for William to be there but with snow now on the mountains she knew the journey would be too hazardous for him to make and she would have to be content to wait for the spring.

On Sunday 1st January 1797 Ann carried her baby the short distance along the track from the farm to the little church of St John the Baptist at Myndtown and there, surrounded by her family, Sarah Howells was christened at the old stone font near the back of the church. Her father's name was not on her baptismal record.

She had William's dark hair and brown eyes and when Ann placed her in the crib that generations of her family had been rocked to sleep in, she sang sweet lullabies that she had learnt from her mother. She dreamed of the day when William would come at last and see his baby daughter.

One March day when the clouds were racing overhead William finally came.

Ann heard the horses come into the yard and looking down from her bedroom through the tiny dormer window she could see William dismounting. She rushed down the wooden stairs.

"William, William, at last you are here. I have been so longing for you to come."

He took her in his arms and they embraced each other but finally she gently pushed him away and with a smile and a brightness in her eyes said,

"Now come in. There is someone very special waiting to meet you." She took his hand and pulling him behind her led him to the crib placed near the fire. "Here is your little daughter, Sarah." William bent over and looked down at the baby and there was such joy in his face. He touched her tiny hand with his big rough one and the baby's eyes opened wide as she gripped his fingers. Ann carefully picked her up,

"You can hold her William, she won't break."

"I've never held a baby before. What do I do?"

"Just bend your arm, like so and I'll place her there." And then they were settled and William was talking to his daughter and telling her how he had come a long way to see her. She looked at him and he looked at her and smiled and told her what a special baby she was. Ann gazed on in sweet contentment. For the first time in her life she felt completely fulfilled. Here she was at last with her man and her child.

That summer proceeded as had the one the previous year. William was besotted with his daughter and tried to visit more often and to stay a little longer each time. It was hard to tear himself away and thoughts of giving up the drover's life and settling down did enter his head. "Just one more year," he'd say to Ann, "then maybe I'll settle down."

By the time of William's last visit of the year Ann knew that she was pregnant again. This baby would be born in the spring.

The winter of 1798 was a harsh one and the snow was still deep on the ground in the middle of February when Ann fell heavily as she went to collect the eggs. Within a few hours she had gone prematurely into labour. Her son was a tiny, underweight baby and at that time of year his chances of survival were poor. He was given his father's name of William when he was christened on the 25th February. A week later on the 4th of March he died. Ann was devastated by the death of her son, the son William had so much hoped for.

When he arrived six weeks later on the first drove of the year he found Ann a changed woman. Where was the bright-eyed girl he had fallen in love with he thought sadly? Her hopes of giving him a son had faded away like the petals of a beautiful flower. But would she blossom again? His daughter was growing fast and was a great joy to him. She was now able to take a few unsteady steps and was attempting to say a few words.

"I'm your Da," he would say to her.

"Da, da, da," she smiled up at him.

He took Ann tenderly in his arms. "My love, there will be other babies. I will come again soon and we will love again and again." He lifted her chin with the tips of his fingers and kissed her long and passionately. He held her to him in one last tender embrace. Ann lifted Sarah up as William rode out of the yard. "Wave bye-bye to your Da." she said.

"Da, da, da," Sarah cooed as she waved her chubby little hand.

Tragically that was the last time Ann saw William. She waited and waited all through the summer but he did not come. Her heart ached for him.

Where was he? What had happened to him?

Finally as the summer drew to a close news of him came. One of the drovers came to her and told of a robbery. William had been carrying a lot of money as the drovers often did. He had been waylaid some miles north of Hereford and been viciously attacked and robbed. A passing farmer had taken him to a nearby house where they had tried to save his life but all to no avail. William had died without regaining consciousness. Ann held her small daughter to her as the tears rolled down her face.

"Your Da is dead my little one. He won't be coming back to us."

"Da, da, da." Sarah murmured.

Ann loved her daughter dearly and, as her mother had done, Sarah learnt the ways of the farm and the rhythms of the year; springtime and lambing; summer and haymaking; autumn and harvesting. Together they walked on the Long Mynd and Sarah never tired of hearing tales of her father, the drover. And Ann never tired of talking of him, the one true love of her life.

Her brother Thomas married Mary in 1810 and they came to live at the farm. Ann's father was glad to have his son there to help with the sheep and gradually as he became an old man his son took over the running of the farm. Ann and Mary became good friends and as Mary had a baby every other year, soon the place was vibrant with life again.

In due course when she was about fourteen Sarah left the farm and became a servant in Bishops Castle a few miles away. She was able to go back frequently and see her mother and her many cousins.

In 1822 at Kerry Church she made a good marriage to Evan Watkin, a moderately wealthy farmer and miller and they lived at Goitre Mill near Kerry. They had ten children although not all of them survived to adulthood. From time to time Sarah would harness the pony and trap and take one or two of her children back to Myndtown to see their grandmother Ann. Once more tales of William the Drover would be told and her grandchildren thought how romantic it all had been and would gaze up at the old drovers' road winding its way through the heather up the side of the Long Mynd.

Thomas and Mary's children were growing up and in time his son took over the farm, married and then more children were born. Ann survived to a great old age and could be found with a shawl round her shoulders in her chair near the fire with her foot rocking the cradle of the latest baby and a gentle smile on her lips as she remembered the love of her life so long ago.

****

By 1851 Evan Watkin was still the miller at Goitre and was also farming sixty-five acres. His sons Edward and Thomas were working for him as were his daughters Ann and Sarah. His younger daughters Jane and Matilda were still at school as was another son, Evan.

But all was to change dramatically in 1855 when Sarah's husband Evan died. He had recently moved from Goitre Mill and had taken on the mill at Penygelli, near Sarn. Sarah valiantly became the miller, aided by her twenty-six year old son Thomas who had been his father's right hand man for several years. Jane, Matilda and Evan were still living and helping at home and there were four servants as well.

The year after Evan died their daughter Ann married and went to live in Shrewsbury where she had two children. Her marriage was tragically cut short by her husband's death in 1861. By now the railway had reached Kerry and Sarah was able to go to her daughter in Shrewsbury. She stayed with her for a while but then returned to Penygelli Mill where she was still the miller at the age of seventy-five. In the next few years she gradually went blind and in 1881 she was living on the hills above the village of Sarn with her daughter Jane at the hamlet of Bahaithlon. Like her mother Ann she too lived to a grand old age and was eighty-six when she died. She is buried in Sarn Churchyard.

Sarah's son Thomas became a full time farmer and married Ann in 1862. Her daughter Mary married Edward Benbow in 1857 and lived in Oswestry. Matilda married John Pugh and had a large family and they continued to live in and around Kerry.

But it was Sarah's daughter, Sarah Watkin, who travelled the furthest away from where she had been born in Kerry, Montgomeryshire in 1836 and where she had been baptised on 7th February in Kerry Church. She went to Birmingham where she found work as a housemaid, married and raised a family. She will appear again later in the story.

There were other travellers over half a century earlier who had come much, much further than Sarah and the lives of whose descendants, like hers, would become inextricably bound together.

Chapter Three

The Journey Back

Ann pulled her cloak round her shoulders, held Margaret firmly on her lap, and peered between the gaps in the canvas. Memories from her childhood flooded through her; memories of the tales her grandmother had told her that she had heard at her mother's knee of ancestors having to leave Herefordshire at the time of the English Civil war when the Puritans had been persecuted; memories of its beauty and of the gently flowing River Wye.

"Look William, we're not far off now. This must be the beautiful River Wye and the old stone bridge just before the town. We're nearly there!" She felt so excited.

2. The Old Bridge over the River Wye, Hereford

The lumbering wagon bumped and rattled slowly along and Ann and William were very thankful that their long journey from America was nearly at an end. She felt a strange sense of homecoming. Her ancestors had known this landscape with its rolling hills, green fields and orchards and now she would get to know it too.

William Saint ran his hands through his shoulder length fair hair, scratched at several days growth of beard and stretched his stiff and bruised limbs as much as he could in the confined space and anticipated the relief he would feel at being let out of this uncomfortable wagon. "I'll have to look for work when we get there as our money will soon be gone," he mused.

"William, I'm longing for our own home where we won't continually be reviled every time we go outside and where we can live in peace with our neighbours and bring up our children in a fair society."

Ann's ancestors had been farmers and Puritans and had gone to the New World to seek a better life away from persecution. Some had overcome the hardships that settling into a new country had involved but some had not survived the hunger, the cold and the hostility of the natives.

But after that initial period had passed, life for succeeding generations had improved until the unrest of the Colonists had erupted into open hostility with what became known as the Boston Tea Party, a political demonstration in 1773 against being taxed by the British Government without having any representation in that Parliament. Settlers disguised themselves as Indians and ruined a whole consignment of the East India Company tea by throwing it into Boston Harbour on the east coast of America. The turmoil that followed developed into the War of Independence that was won in 1783 by the Colonists who wanted to be independent of England and its Parliament.

William was a Loyalist, loyal to the British crown. Having served his apprenticeship as a boot and shoemaker before the war he put his skills to good use by making boots and scabbards for a foot regiment during the war. Many people, like William and Ann, had ended up on the losing side; some had gone north to Canada, some to the Bahamas, others returned to England.

Most of the people who had left had gone in the early years soon after the war ended in 1783; William was possibly born in Williamsburg in about 1759. His and Ann's families had remained in Virginia hoping that time would heal the wounds and that they would be integrated into American society. Sadly it had not proved to be the case and there was still a great deal of bitterness. It was against this background that they fell in love and married at the end of the decade.

Ann couldn't understand why people didn't accept them for what they were, just a shoemaker and his wife. Now it was shoemaker, wife and child, for baby Margaret had been born in 1791.

"Enough is enough William, Ann had said, "before we have any more children I want to be in England and I want to go before Margaret starts toddling around because she will be easier to manage on the journey before she starts walking."

"That's a very defeatist attitude Ann. Our forebears didn't come out here for us to run home, tail between our legs, at the first spot of trouble."

"William, a war isn't a spot of trouble. It's a major incident. And I think it's very unfair of you to say we're turning tail at the first spot of trouble anyway. We've stuck this out for nearly ten years now. And still people refuse to speak to us. Imagine what it's going to be like when Margaret goes to school. She won't understand what it's all about. And think about your business. I know you are getting in some orders for boots but in a place without this hostility you could do even better." William turned away angrily; he hated arguments.

"I'll think it over," he said tersely.

Ann went into their small garden with a smile on her face. She had recognised that William was weakening and that her line of argument was gaining strength. She knew better than to press her point too far just now.

Before long the decision was made to leave America and go to England. They bundled up their belongings and prepared themselves for the long sea journey. Ann put aside thoughts of the discomforts of the journey and kept in front of her the thought of her new home in Hereford, of William building up a shoemaking business and family life with Margaret and other, as yet unborn children.

In early summer they obtained passage on a boat travelling to Bristol. As the ropes were cast off and the sails hoisted up the tall masts William and Ann with Margaret in her arms, stood on the deck watching the sails began to fill with a light breeze. As the ship slipped away from its mooring and they began to draw away from the coast William said, "So that's goodbye to America. No going back now. That part of our lives is over. I hope you have no regrets and are prepared for the hardships of this journey."

"William there is just one thing in my mind and that is our new life."

As the wind picked up in the coming days Ann did have more than one thing on her mind as the ship tossed and rolled and went high on the huge waves and descended into the deep troughs. She fought seasickness and sometimes fear but if there were moments when she wished herself on dry land she pushed them away from her and in her mind's eye formed a picture of what she imagined Hereford would be like. Again tales of the beauty of Herefordshire that she had heard in her childhood came to mind and took away her fear.

The cargo in the hold of their ship was tobacco, picked by slaves on the plantations in Virginia; maybe the very slaves that had travelled packed tightly like pickled salted herrings and shackled in leg irons in the same dark, airless hold after they had been brutally captured in Africa. The thought of such cruelty and that as many as four hundred slaves may have spent anything from six weeks or more down there made Ann shudder when she realised the human misery that had gone on in that boat.

On board there was room for a few passengers and travelling with them was a plantation owner and his wife paying a visit to England. They were taking two of their

Negro house servants with them. Their slaves were kind and smiled at Margaret with wide smiles showing lovely white, shiny teeth in their black faces. Margaret was fascinated by them and Ann was pleased to find that during the long, tedious journey they were happy to look after Margaret and play with her for hours at a time.

William was thrilled by the month long voyage across the Atlantic Ocean. They were lucky not to encounter any serious storms and once Ann became used to the movement of the vessel she began to enjoy the journey. It took her a while to get her sea legs, as the ship was almost constantly moving. For most of the time there was a fair wind and the big sails billowed full of air. The ship made good time even though there were a few days when no wind blew and the sails were slack and the ship was becalmed.

After a month at sea, each day there were more sea birds circling round the ship and the captain assured them that this was a sign that they would see land very soon. Several times a day a look out was sent up to the crow's nest to search the horizon for a grey smudge that would indicate that land was ahead.

On the thirtieth day after leaving America they heard the welcome shout from the lookout in the crow's nest "Land Ahoy!" And the next day even the passengers down on the level of the deck could see a line of hills on the horizon.

"Not much longer and we shall be in Bristol," the captain assured them as they stood on the deck looking at some hills in the distance, "those are the Devon hills and if you look the other way you can just see the coast of Wales.

Hereford, where you are going, is beyond there inland and between fifty and sixty miles from the coast."

"Oh William, "Ann said," I can hardly believe that this is happening. That I'm going back to where my ancestors had their home."

The next day there was land on both sides of them as they sailed up the Bristol Channel.

"The ship is going more slowly now we're in more sheltered waters." William observed.

The captain who was nearby said,

"We're helped by the large tidal range here in the Severn estuary and when the tide comes in, it's fast and helps to push the ship forward. Sometimes we have to anchor when the tide's falling so we don't get swept out to sea again." And later he said to them, "We'll soon be at the mouth of the River Avon and then we wait for a rising tide to push the ship eight miles up the river to Bristol."

At the entrance to the River Avon they took on a pilot who knew the channel well. Mostly the wind would not help them so there were several teams of men known as 'hobblers' in rowing boats who would attach lines to the ship and would tow it up to the port.

Although the tide helped the ship up the river, when it went down again the ships were stranded on the mud in the harbour. It was important to disembark the passengers quickly while the boats were still upright. Unless the boats were tied up tightly they could keel over to one side. Some cargoes had been spilt onto the mud and into the water and this was beginning to make Bristol less popular as a port but within a few years lock gates were built to hold the water in the harbour when the tide went down so that the ships remained afloat, but that was a few years after William and Ann's journey in 1792.

When they sailed into the crowded harbour ropes were flung out to the men who stood on the quayside to guide the ship safely in among all the other tall ships and finally they were tied up. They hurriedly disembarked from the boat and stood with their boxes and bundles around them on the bustling quayside. This was the first time for weeks that they had stood on firm land, it felt so strange, just as if they were still on board a swaying ship.

Ann put a protective arm round little Margaret who was clinging to her skirts, baffled by all the strange noises and activities going on around her. While William rammed his broad brimmed felt hat on his head and went off to find a man who could take them to a tavern for the night she looked around her at the multitude of masts belonging to the ships tied up at the quayside, at the merchants shouting instructions about the cargo and at barrels and boxes being unloaded by burly men.

When William returned with a man and a cart their belongings were piled onto it, he took Margaret in his arms and they followed on through the maze of streets surrounding the harbour.

The following morning they started the journey of many miles by carrier's cart on rough roads; at first to Gloucester and then on through Ross-on-Wye to Hereford. There were stops during the day for the horses to be changed; they were able to get down and walk around to stretch their legs gratefully and overnight they slept at wayside inns. The journey was long and tedious but Ann knew that in the end it would all have been worthwhile. Finally, as the wagon rumbled over the ancient bridge and into Hereford Ann caught a glimpse of the cathedral and knew that at the first opportunity she would return to look again at the river and to explore the town. The weary travellers climbed stiffly down from the wagon. Ann held Margaret as William helped to unload their boxes. The hour was late and they were pleased to obtain lodging for the night and a meal at a nearby tavern.

The following morning while William went to several shoemakers in the town to seek work Ann tucked her dark hair into a kerchief , pulled her cloak round her and took Margaret by the hand and led the toddler down to the ancient stone bridge they had crossed the night before. As people, wagons and carriages hurried past them Ann drew Margaret in beside her to the comparative safety of the V shaped passing places set back in the walls of the bridge. Beneath them the water swirled through the arches and on the banks of the river cargo was loaded and unloaded from the many sloops that plied their trade between Hereford and Gloucester.

When Margaret became bored with looking at the boats they retraced their steps into the town. Ann wanted to see the famous cathedral but from the view of it she had seen from the bridge there appeared to be something very wrong with it indeed. It looked more like a ruin. As Margaret had not been walking for long they made slow progress with Ann having to pick her up and carry her at frequent intervals. They climbed up Gwynne Street and as they came nearer to the cathedral Ann could see a scene of devastation. The western end was indeed a ruin and there was fallen masonry everywhere. She was staring at it in amazement when a passer-by noticed her.

"Looks like you are a stranger here missus."

"Yes I am and I'm wondering what has happened here?"

"There was a terrible disaster here on Easter Monday in 1786 when the West Tower collapsed. As you can see it brought down the West Front and part of the nave as well."

"It's an absolute ruin isn't it? I've been so much looking forward to seeing the wonderful cathedral and now I cannot."

"Well one day it will be restored but it will take years and years and will cost a huge amount of money.

Margaret was beginning to grizzle because she was getting hungry so Ann picked her up and walked back through the town to their lodging. Soon after they arrived a jubilant William returned.

"Ann there are several boot and shoe makers in this town, more than one in St Owen Street alone and at one of them I managed to get taken on as an assistant. The owner could see I was a hard worker when I showed him the callouses on my hands. He's getting on in years and his wife wants him to stop living over the shop and take on an assistant so I arrived at just the right time. Furthermore there is living accommodation for us there and when he moves out there will be more. So what do you think?"

"It sounds perfect. When do we move in?"

"Let's go just as soon as we've had a bite to eat and then we can see what needs doing."

Half an hour later William strode quickly along carrying Margaret in his strong arms. Ann struggled to keep up with them as they went back through High Town and down into St Owen Street. A few doors along on the left William stopped. "Here it is, let's go in."

Ann looked at the sign above the front of the shop, 'Richard Prosser. Cobbler' and smiled up at her husband, "This is our new life beginning William. It looks good."

Together they entered the shoemaker's shop. Ann looked about her at the sheets of leather and breathed in the well-remembered smell. Along the length of one wall a shelf was crowded with wooden lasts of different sizes. On a bench beneath them were the shoemaker's tools, knives for cutting the leather, awls for making the holes, strong thread for sewing the leather together, hammers, marking wheels and stretching pliers. Mr Prosser, elderly and somewhat bent, moved forward to greet them as they came through the doorway. He had been working at the back of the shop where large windows let in the light

"Good day to you Ma'am. So this is your fair lady, William, and your little one. They look bonny. And you've had a long journey across the sea to get here. I hope in Hereford you will find everything you want and be happy."

"Thank you sir, I'm relieved to have that journey behind us and to be here at last."

"Your William and I talked about the work here this morning so I expect you'd like to meet my missus and have a look at where you'll be living. Now these stairs are very steep, so mind how you go and William watch out for those low beams."

"Can I hear voices coming up the stairs?" called out Mrs Prosser.

"Yes here's William, my new worker and his wife and child."

"Oh please call me Ann and this is Margaret."

"We're very pleased to see you Ann and that's a very pretty little girl. Your William came along just at the right time. Now come and have a look at where you'll be living for the time being though before long we shall move out and you'll have more room. There's no need for me to come, but you just go on up those stairs and what you see is yours to do what you want with; so go along with you and have a look at it and see if it will do".

They went up another flight of steep stairs and emerged at the top into two attic rooms with small dormer windows let into the roof. "Oh William come and have a look. If you crane your head out just so you can see the street far below us and over the roof tops you can see right out into the countryside."

William stood behind her and put his hands on her shoulders. "Turn around Ann and look at these rooms. What do you think?"

"The stairs are steep and the rooms are dusty but it's nothing a good sweep and scrub won't put right. We can put up a bed for us over there with Margaret on a truckle bed at the side of us. There's a fireplace in the other room so we can cook on that. It's a long way to carry water up for washing but we'll manage. At least when we go along the street we won't have people calling out rude things to us. I'm just so glad to be here."

"So am I," said William, "shall I go down and ask Mrs Prosser if she'll lend us a broom and then we can start cleaning it up and maybe move in tomorrow?" Later that afternoon the rooms had been cleaned and William had found wood that he could knock together for a slatted bed for them and he could fetch straw to fill a mattress. He made a little bed for Margaret that would push underneath theirs during the day.

The next day they borrowed a handcart and piled all their possessions onto it and trundled along to St Owen Street. Mrs Prosser looked after Margaret while Ann and William puffed up and down the two flights of stairs with bedding, pots and pans, clothes and the rest of their meagre possessions.

William started work the next day and was glad to be doing what he knew so well. He handled the leather and familiar tools confidently and was soon choosing the lasts, cutting out the shapes; making holes with an awl and threading a strong needle with the waxed thread getting ready to stitch up his first shoe. Mr Prosser dealt with the customers as they came to be measured for shoes or to pay for a pair that had been completed. William could see why he needed an assistant. If you were serving customers all the time you'd never get the shoes made.

3. Shop in Hereford where William may have worked

Upstairs in the attic Ann settled in and arranged and re-arranged their few possessions while Margaret played on the floor and when it was time to go shopping Mrs Prosser went with her to show her the market and the best places to buy everything she needed.

So Ann and William entered into a period of great happiness in their lives. They were young and their new life was everything they hoped it would be. William worked hard and was highly thought of by Richard Prosser. He soon realised that he could completely trust William and leave him in charge of the shop when necessary.

A few months later Ann was delighted to find that she was pregnant again. The Prossers moved out in the early spring to a small house on the edge of the town, so by the time baby Ann was born there was only one flight of stairs to go up most of the time as they had moved one floor down to occupy the larger rooms on the first floor. Ann was baptised at All Saints Church on 6th May 1794. Two years later another daughter was born to them and at her baptism at All Saints Church on the 2nd October 1796 she was named Elizabeth.

Ann couldn't help contrasting their busy life now with the last few months in America where they had struggled to make a living as they had so few customers. Within a few years Mr Prosser had handed the shop over to William completely and William took on two more workers. Business was growing, and so was their family. Thomas was born in 1799 and was baptised at the church of St John the Baptist on January 1st 1800 and then James in 1802; he was baptised at the same church on 28th January.

In the following years William and Ann became completely integrated into the life of Hereford. The shop thrived and William took on apprentices, the children grew up and it was almost unimaginable that they had once lived so far away over the sea. William went into a partnership with James Gore and Thomas Williams to buy some land and buildings just outside where St Owen's Gate had once been. This was an astute investment in a growing town for when they sold the land again in the summer of 1806 they made a good profit.

On 11th December 1811 Margaret, who as a very small

child had travelled across the ocean from America, married Job Blick at St Peter's Church at the top end of St Owen Street. Subsequently they went to live in Kidderminster where Job was a carpet maker. Thomas became a brick maker at Holmer on the outskirts of Hereford and married Susannah Clarke in about 1819. James became an apprentice baker, later having his own shop in St Martin Street and eventually a shop in St Owen Street. He married Ellen Bailey in 1821.

In 1823 William died and was buried in St Owen's graveyard. Ann may have run the shop herself for a while but eventually she went to live with her son Thomas at the end of St Owen Street, once the location of the old town gate. She survived William for many years; on the 10th April 1840 she died of paralysis aged eighty.

In 1837 William and Ann's granddaughter Mary, daughter of their son Thomas, was born and she now takes up the family story.

.

Chapter Four

Part One

The Hereford Years

I think it must have been my grandmother, Ann Saint, who had held the family together in the early years. She was an indomitable lady. Sadly I don't remember her as I was only three when she died in 1840 but I would have loved to have heard the exciting tales she had to tell of her early years in America with Grandfather William. They came to Hereford where Grandfather had a cobblers shop near the top end of St Owen Street. It was taken over by another cobbler later and was there for many years and may still be a cobblers shop for all I know. So I had to rely on my older brother John to pass on what he could remember of her stories and by the time he was able to talk to me even more years had passed and memories were growing dim.

My parents were Thomas Saint and his wife Susannah. They were married in Hereford in 1819 and they named their first daughter Ann after our Grandmother, but Ann died when she was fifteen, two years before I was born and I never did find out what she died from. Illness was rife and many people died young. I spent my childhood and early years in Hereford where in 1841 my mother's life, after repeated pregnancies had haemorrhaged away following the birth of her last still born child. My father died of tuberculosis in Hereford Workhouse two years

later when I was six but I now need to go back before that
to tell you about my family and then to explain how our
family life disintegrated.

My brother John was born in 1821 and when he was old
enough to work he was a brick maker like our father.
They'd put up some bread and cheese for midday and
tramp off together to the brickfields at Holmer nearly two
miles away. It was a lovely walk along lanes and footpaths
in spring when the fresh green leaves were on the trees and
the banks of the lanes were covered in primroses. In the
summer months the meadows were full of wildflowers and
bees buzzed around collecting pollen and nectar.
Butterflies danced in the warm air and nestlings poked
their yellow beaks up waiting for their parents to return
with tasty mouthfuls. At haymaking time the air was
fragrant with the cut grass. In late summer there were ripe
apples on trees that overhung the hedgerows and
blackberries that could be picked on the way home.

In the winter it was still dark when they set off and it was
harsh when the rain or snow was in their faces as they
trudged along; it was cold and wet when they got there as
well and it was heavy work making bricks. Eventually my
father was too ill to walk to Holmer and too ill to work at
all.

But before that they were not alone tramping along the
lanes. Other brick makers were making their way to
Holmer and farm workers were hurrying along to get to
the farms early to milk the cows. The Hereford cattle
market was famous throughout the area and quite often
they encountered the drovers who came down from the

Welsh hills with their black cattle to buy more beasts and then walk them all onwards to the markets in the English Midlands, the South and to London.

Farmers' wives would pass them on the road, their carts loaded with milk, butter, eggs and vegetables and there were flagons of cider safely stowed under the seats. They were hurrying to get into town to set up their stalls and, if there was time, to have a good gossip with the other women about the goings on in the farming world, until the housewives of Hereford came along with their baskets that they would fill with butter and cheese, eggs and vegetables and the produce from the Herefordshire countryside.

Thomas and Susannah's second daughter was Elizabeth, born in 1823. She was fourteen years older than me so seemed a very grown up sister. Her husband, James Wilmot, and their first son Samuel were brick makers too and they lived on Brick Road near the canal. Her children were only a few years younger than I was.

After Elizabeth came Thomas and Susannah's next two children. Thomas, born in 1825 was named after our father but, like our sister Ann born in 1820, he died in 1835. Maybe there was a cholera outbreak that year or some other disease leading to the loss of two children in one year but anything was possible in the part of the town that we lived in near to where St Owen's Gate had once been. There were open ditches close by into which any old rubbish was thrown including human waste. It didn't smell good either. In fact it stank.

William and Sophia were born next in 1827 and 1829 but in the turmoil of my early years I completely lost touch with them. I always imagined William might have gone to sea and I suppose that Sophia like other young girls of our class went into service and then maybe married but I just don't know. With hindsight it seems sad to me that we can so easily lose contact with our kith and kin.

Thomas and Susannah's four youngest children were all girls and included me so apart from big brother John they were the ones I was closest to.

Charlotte, born in 1831, was ten when our mother died so with our father's health being what it was her fate was the same as mine until she was fourteen when she became a servant. That didn't suit her for long, and who can blame her, so she got herself a lodging with Maryanne Barlow a hawker who lived in Gaol Lane. She became a charwoman and later married John Bishop and they had several children. He subsequently became a labourer in an iron works in Tipton so she found herself living in the Black Country not far away from me in Birmingham. But all that was many years after the time I am now recounting. Jane, born in 1832, was surrounded by a certain amount of notoriety and I will have plenty to say about her later.

Then there was Catherine who was just two years older than me so we were very close which made what happened to her very hard for me to bear. She and I were tossed about in life's storm probably more than the others as we were so young when disaster struck our family. We lived in what I think must have been the poorest part of the town. It was at the end of St Owen Street near to where one of the old gateways into the city had been. The gateway had been demolished in 1782.

With our father being such a lowly labourer at the brick works, money was always a problem and we lived in very cramped quarters, in part of what was called Lambs Buildings at the back of the Lamb Tavern of which George Russell was the landlord when we lived there.

4. Lambs Buildings, Hereford

Close by in the streets at the back were the Workhouse and the Gaol, but more pleasantly going the other way we could walk down Cantilupe Street and Mill Lane to reach the River Wye. When I was very young you could still see the sloops taking passengers and goods down to Gloucester on the river. I was about seven when the canal finally reached Hereford and then goods travelled by barge down to Gloucester through Ledbury. At the end of Mill Lane there was once the Castle Mill but both it and the Castle are long gone, although on Cantilupe Street you can see the pond, which is all that remains of the castle moat.

There is a pleasant grassy area above the river where the castle once stood and there is the monument to Nelson that commemorates his victory at the Battle of Trafalgar. He had been made a freeman of Hereford in 1802 and was very popular all over England. When he was killed three years later at Trafalgar it was decided to erect a monument to him on Castle Green with a statue of him on the top. Eventually after they'd got so far with the monument the money ran out and instead of a statue there was just an urn at the top of the stone column.

5. The Nelson Monument, Hereford

Before I continue with my personal story I must mention

our Uncle James and his family who lived further up St
Owen Street at a much more respectable address in the
gentrified part of the street. Uncle James, a baker, was our
father's younger brother. Around the time I was born he
moved from his first shop in St Martin's Street to much
better premises in St Owen Street.

Not for him the long daily trudge, whatever the weather,
to the brickfield like our father, or the long hours spent in
the cold, wet and dirt once he got there. He lived above
the shop and had to get up in the middle of the night to
start mixing the dough, leave it to prove, then shape it into
loaves and bake it. From my very early childhood I loved
the warmth in his shop and the smell of freshly baked
loaves that spread into the street and sometimes the rare
chance to taste the warm crusty bread. Even as a very
small child I'd make my way along the street to where he
lived. You could smell the delicious aroma coming out of
the shop long before you got there. I'd push the door open
and there was the jovial figure of Uncle James enveloped
in his big white apron. His booming voice would call out,
"Here's my little angel come to see her Uncle James." And
then he'd give me a big hug and leave me covered in flour.
Aunt Ellen was a shadowy figure in the background,
probably with a glass in her hand.

"Just something to keep me going," she'd say to me, her
words sometime strangely slurred. Of course I had no idea
what was going on.

"Let's see if we can find something for you," Uncle would
say and then he'd hand me a sticky bun or a piece of new
bread. What a treat that was. Then I got out from under

his feet and out of the way of the customers coming into the shop and I'd sit on the flagstones outside in the sun and lean against the warm wall. In the spring he had wallflowers in a pot by the shop door. I can remember now the wonderful scent coming from them and the bees buzzing around collecting nectar as I sat there enjoying my bun.

He'd married Aunt Ellen in 1821 and I suspect that their first child may have been on the way at the time of the wedding for Aunt Ellen was only sixteen. But then there's nothing strange about that, it happens all the time. Their children's ages were very similar to those in our family and their last child, Ellen, was just three years younger than me.

It may have been a case of 'marry in haste, repent at leisure' as far as Aunt Ellen was concerned or was it the strange hours that Uncle James worked? That's as it maybe but as the years went on I came to realise that she'd taken to drink so although I compared the working lives and conditions of the two brothers somewhat disparagingly, his married life was not without its problems. He had demanding working hours and eight children to bring up so a wife who was close friends with the gin bottle put a lot of strain on the marriage. Eventually she died of delirium tremens when I was ten. This could explain why he was unable to do much to help us when our difficulties became so acute, although he was generous with loaves of bread when we asked for them.

His son William, who had been a baker's apprentice, married Elizabeth Walters in 1846 when he was twenty-one. Obviously the idea of being a baker didn't suit him and he had become a policeman in Hereford but sometime after the marriage they left Hereford and he became a policeman in London. His mother Ellen, died the year after William's marriage. When he was an old man, a widower and a police pensioner he returned to live out his days in Hereford where his daughter Mary, who had worked as a cook in London, cared for him.

Two years after Aunt Ellen died Uncle James married again. His new wife was only two years older than William. In 1849 a son Charles was born to them. Another of Uncle James's sons was named after him and became a baker but sadly he died in the Infirmary at the workhouse of a brain disease when he was only twenty-nine in 1861; but I had already left Hereford by then.

My brother John had to assume the mantle of head of the family some time before our father died because he, poor man, was ill for a long time prior to his death. In the following years I was close to John who did his best to look after the younger members of the family despite his limited means. But he'd had his own share of family tragedy. His little son William died in 1843 when he was only a few months old and his first wife Eliza died in 1845 a few months after giving birth to their daughter Eliza. But within a few years he had married Maryanne and later they had a son called John.

It was probably when our father became so ill and we were desperate for food that Jane started stealing. I expect at that time it was at the market that there were the greatest opportunities among the crowds of people thronging round the stalls. She was only about nine and I don't suppose anyone took her petty thieving seriously. Maybe her arm would stretch forward between the shoppers and a hand would grab a piece of fruit, a loaf of bread or a lump of cheese. And if any one did notice her she was nimble of foot and ran off quickly down one of the narrow streets and passageways near the Cathedral and got away before anyone could catch her. She had realised early on how easy it was to steal and to get away with it and there were serious consequences of this early stealing a few years later.

Catherine and I were too young to realise what was happening and all we knew was that some days there was food and some days there was none and most days we were cold and dirty. Eventually Father became far too ill to work or look after us in any way. He was coughing up blood all the time and was a pitiful sight to see. Either John or the landlord of The Lamb notified the authorities, for finally the Poor Law Union sent the Relieving Officer who came to the dirty, impoverished and unsanitary rooms we lived in behind The Lamb Inn to see what help, if any, might be given to us.

"Who is this stranger who has come here?" I remember asking Charlotte.

"Hush Mary" she replied, "He's come to see if he can help us."

The man must have taken just one look at our feverish father holding a spittoon and lying on his bed of rags in the corner and then seen the dirty, unkempt and starving condition of the rest of us for he judged us to be in need of immediate help.

"You're in a bad way here mister," he said to father, "Can anyone in your family take you in?"

"No, there is no one."

"Well in that case I'm giving you this ticket so you and the children can get help straight way. Take it with you and go to the Workhouse, go today."

The Workhouse was not far away from where we lived so we gathered together our few possessions and Charlotte and Jane helped our poor father to his feet and off we went. It was a sad little procession that straggled along the road that day at the tail end of winter; a few errant snowflakes were drifting about. Catherine and I didn't really understand what was happening other than that it was something very bad. We were crying and holding on to each other. Our father was very troubled by what had befallen us.

"My poor children," he said, "life has been very bad to us since your dear mother died. Now we are quite destitute and this is the only way. But there will be a bright future. Have no fear."

There was no bright future for him or for any of us. But perhaps he could have been talking of his imminent death, as in only a few short months he would leave his earthly body and be free of his worldly woes.

We approached the workhouse with quaking legs. Everyone spoke of it as being the last place on earth you would wish to end up in. Even at six years old I could feel the sense of dread with which people had spoken of 'The

Workhouse'. It was a cold March day when I went through the Porter's lodge. There were two entrances, one for males and one for females. It was many long years before I came through it again to the outside world. And then it was not on the way to freedom but to an equally harsh life elsewhere. I think Charlotte was in there for about two years and Jane for about five years. Catherine spent six or seven years within its walls and I was there for eight years. During those years I was cut off from Jane's life of theft after she went out into the world again and it wasn't until much later that it all came to light. All of us were there until we reached fourteen, the legal age for employment in the outside world.

A few months after that dreadful March day in 1843 we were orphaned. Our father died in June. The Board of Guardians of the Workhouse became our legal guardians until we were fourteen and they were then supposed to check on our welfare until we were sixteen. But on that cold March day none of us had any thought for the future apart from our father with his vain hopes of better days to come. The present was quite bad enough. Never had I wanted my mother as much as I did that day but wanting her was quite hopeless, as she had died two years earlier. I felt very alone and frightened and I know Catherine did too. We lacked any older mother figure in our lives. Uncle James's wife was often too drunk to care about us and brother John's wife was nursing a dying baby. We only had each other to cling to.

But in the meantime the four of us had to get used to the harsh life in the workhouse. The day that we went in was one of unimaginable horror for us. Our clothes were taken from us and we were made to have a bath and were scrubbed quite hard and our hair was washed and cut short. We were then given the distinctive uniform worn by the rest of the inmates. Girls and women wore coarse grogram gowns. There were calico shifts, petticoats of Linsey-Woolsey material, gingham dresses, day caps and worsted stockings. Woven slippers were also provided which to me was luxury as in our destitute state we had often gone barefoot.

Firstly we were put in the relieving ward where we stayed until the medical officer had examined us and we were assessed. That day was the last we ever saw or heard of our poor father until the day we were called to the Matron's office in June to be informed that he had died. So as we were all under fourteen we children were apart from the older women. Many of the children there were orphans, as we were soon to become. I found out later that half of the children in workhouses at that time were orphans or had been deserted by their parents. Some were the children of felons or cripples or the insane. They were a motley crew of disturbed and frightened children for the most part and there were a few bullies. However the four of us kept together at first and anyone trying to molest or bully us realised there were two older sisters who would stick up for us.

We were shown the dormitory where we would be sleeping. The iron bedsteads were arranged in rows in what appeared to me to be a huge room. The building had only been open for about five years so the straw mattresses, sheets and blankets were not as worn out as they would become later. That first night was very frightening with so many strange children in the room. Some of them were playing up and jumping over the beds even when there was a child trying to sleep in one. When finally everybody had settled down some of the children were having nightmares or crying for their mothers. I felt like crying for mine but Catherine and I were sharing a bed so we cuddled up to each other and that gave us both some comfort. Sometimes there were three or even four children to a bed but you don't expect the luxury of a bed to yourself when you go to the workhouse and anyway many children were used to sleeping three or more to a bed before they went there.

The next morning breakfast time was another shock. All the children sat in rows at trestle tables and we had a bowl of thin porridge and a piece of bread and this was what we had every day. Some people complained about it not being enough but so recently there had been days for us without any food that I was grateful for what we did have. We had to eat in silence and the punishment for breaking that rule or any of the others was to be caned or flogged or to be locked in a room on your own. It was against the rules to beat girls but I think it went on sometimes. There was also a rule that no male child over fourteen should be flogged but younger boys were flogged and it was very cruel. The mealtimes certainly became monotonous with little variation day in day out. There was thin gruel and bread, sometimes a little tough meat, sometimes some cheese. But it was better than starving and we were clothed and shod.

There was three hours schooling for us every day. We were taught to read and write and do arithmetic. The principles of the Christian religion were drummed into us. I heard later that there were some complaints from people outside who said we were getting a better free education than children outside whose education had to be paid for. In later life I met plenty of poor people who could neither read nor write so my years in the workhouse had given me some advantages although it was a hard way to get them.

We were also prepared for our life after our time in the workhouse was over. For boys there were training and apprenticeships for trades like tailoring or shoemaking and we girls were taught how to sew and do laundry and the skills necessary for housekeeping. The workhouse had gardens where we worked as we became older, to grow the vegetables and fruit that added to our diet or were sold to make money for the workhouse. Pigs were kept and these also were sold at market or slaughtered for use within the workhouse kitchens.

If this all sounds good training for our future lives I don't deny that but it was the spirit of the place that was so disheartening. There was a lot of cruelty and deprivation but we children knew that there was a good chance that when we left the workhouse at the age of fourteen we would go into work, which for girls was likely to mean going into service or for boys taking up some trade. However for the many adults there they were hard times indeed. Their work included stone crushing, picking oakum and sorting hair. There was also work for them in the extensive vegetable gardens and in the piggery. The women worked in the laundry, helped with the cooking and scrubbed floors.

One by one my sisters departed into the outside world when they became fourteen and were old enough to be legally employed. Charlotte went first after having been inside for about two years and then two or three years later Jane went out. As the time drew near for Catherine to go out into the world she began to feel very sad about leaving me, aged twelve, behind and at the same time fearful of what her future would be. She became morose and I would try to cheer her up by saying, "It's only another eighteen months to two years for me Catherine. I know it seems a long time but it will pass just as all these other long, interminable years have done."

"Yes Mary but you will be here on your own and we've always been together. You will be lonely in this dreadful place."

"I'll spend the time looking forward to when we can be together again and although we'll both be servants with limited time off at least when we are free we can do what we want to do and go where we want to go. Now do try to cheer up. Soon you will be able to visit our brother John again and go and see if Uncle James has any nice buns."

So the day finally came. She was fourteen in August and by November she had become a servant for a Mister Phillips and his wife. He was a cordwainer. When we made our farewells I had no sense of foreboding of what the future had in store. Very little news filtered in from the outside world so I had to wait for the full story to unfold when I went out nearly two years later. But before that there was the dreadful and shocking March day when I was summoned to leave my work and go to the Matron's room. She was in a foul mood, which was not unusual so as I stood there waiting for her to speak I wracked my brains for some misdeed I must have unknowingly committed. Nothing could have prepared me for the shock I felt when she finally glared at me and barked,

"So your useless, good for nothing sister Catherine is dead. She drowned herself in the canal. When I think of all the years we have fed her, clothed her and educated her and the worthless hussy repays us by doing this. Right you can go and when your turn comes to leave don't you dare do what she has done. Off you go, back to your work girl!"

There was no point in asking for more details or if I could go out and see John. I would not have been allowed to go. I just had to keep my misery to myself. And miserable I was. I couldn't really take in that Catherine was no more and that she had actually taken her own life was beyond my comprehension. What on earth had been going on? But as I said none of these questions could be answered until I was once more out in the world and could get all the details from John. So it wasn't until about eighteen months later that I heard the whole story or at least as much of it as will ever be known.

Catherine had left the workhouse in the autumn of 1849 and had gone to be a live-in servant at the home of William Phillips in Bye Street. Also living there were his wife, although by the following year she had died, and his niece, Mary Ann Grainger. There was also a daughter called Martha who was about twenty and a son, also called William.

William Phillips was a cordwainer, employing four men, so

he made shoes just as Grandfather William had done. The son William was a bookseller and had a shop in the High Town. Catherine was a maid of all work so she was at the beck and call of the family all hours of the day, cleaning, laying fires and then at the end of the day she also had to sweep out the shop.

The son William, who had the bookshop in High Town, did not eat his meals at home so another of Catherine's tasks was to take them to him at his shop and then go back later for the empty dishes.

Catherine had told our brother John that William Phillips and his wife were kind to her but Mr Phillips said he had found her sullen and would rarely answer when spoken to although generally her behaviour was good and she was healthy. I then remembered the moroseness she had developed in the last few months of being at the Workhouse and thought it probable that her lowness of spirits had continued.

On one particular Friday near the end of March, in the middle of the morning, Mrs Phillips was in Catherine's bedroom and had to speak to her about 'certain unclean habits' she had developed. The niece, Mary Grainger had also observed these unclean habits and had told Catherine that if she noticed it again she would speak to the Matron of the Workhouse about it. What could this be? Had she not emptied her overnight chamber pot I wondered?

But after that, the day continued as normal with no hint of what was to come and Catherine carried on with her chores and ate her meals as usual. At about five o'clock the niece, Mary Grainger, having prepared her cousin

William's tea, took it to the door and gave it to Catherine to carry to William's shop in the High Town as usual. This she did and then she came back and ate her own tea. Afterwards she went back to the bookshop to collect the tea things returning with them and doing various chores including sweeping out the shop. It seems, according to what was said at the Inquest, that she again set out for the bookshop but in fact did not go there. She went as far as Mr Minton's corner and turned along St Owen Street. Mrs Phillips became alarmed after a while when Catherine had not returned as she never stayed out when on errands. So she set out to look for her. She found that Catherine had not been to the bookshop and when enquiries were made among her friends she discovered that no one had seen her.

That evening a man called Charles Gillett was walking along the canal tow path at about seven o'clock when he saw a shawl and a pinafore floating on the water near Burcott Wharf. He showed them to Mr Ballard, an engineer who lived in nearby Widemarsh Street who suggested he take them to the Workhouse; this he did but they were not claimed there.

The next day, on the Saturday morning, as Catherine was still missing Mr Phillips spoke to Inspector Davies of the Herefordshire police. It was now widely supposed that Catherine was drowned in the canal and John told me that he and William Lewis, a policeman, went to search the canal. William Lewis obtained some drags from the Infirmary and Mr Ballard lent them a punt. When John told me about this, although more than a year had passed, I could see from his face what a dreadful ordeal this had been.

"Mary, we started to drag the canal at the beginning of the tunnel under Ailstone Hill looking for Catherine's body and we went right through to the end of the tunnel but we did not find her." Even as he told me tears were running down my face.

6. The canal where Catherine's body was found

"My poor, poor sister," I murmured, "lying there in the cold water all through that night."

"Poor me as well looking for her, not knowing at any moment what we would find but suspecting the worst."

"Yes, awful for you. A terrible thing to have to do."

"Anyway on we went until about two hundred yards on the River Lugg side of the tunnel we found her. There she was at the bottom of the water, still wearing her gown, shoes and her other items of clothing and her bonnet still tied about her neck." His voice broke, "Oh Mary, it was a terrible sight."

In a few moments he had composed himself again and continued.

"William Lewis and I managed to get her body out of the canal and laid it on the bank wondering what we should do next. He knew the landlord of the nearby inn, The White Swan, so I picked up her cold, wet body and I carried her there with the water from her clothes streaming down my trousers and over my arms. And that is where the inquest was held a few days later. The surgeon, Mr Charles Lingen said he had examined the body and found nothing remarkable about it apart from a slight bruise on the cheek, not enough to suppose that any violence had been used. The verdict was 'Found Drowned'."

"Had she really taken her own life John or were the papers being dramatic as usual hoping to increase their sales?"

"I can't say Mary, I just don't know. There seemed to be

no particular reason why she should do away with herself although according to what Mr Phillips said at the Inquest she was sullen."

7. The Swan Inn, Hereford

"Well I can tell you that before she left the workhouse she had become very low in spirits." And then I continued, "But if she threw herself into the canal at Burcott Wharf where her shawl and pinafore were found how come her body was found over a mile away?"

"Well those items must have been found very soon after she went into the water so there hadn't been time for them to float away. But she was in the water for hours after that and with the water level being high and the strong wind we'd had during the day there must have been quite a current moving along the canal and overnight taking poor

Catherine with it, she was very slight remember. We'll never know the entire truth will we? This is just another sad episode in our family and there have been a great many of those."

8. Catherine's inquest took place in this room

"The Matron of the Workhouse let me know in no uncertain terms that she was an ungrateful hussy and had taken her own life. Of course there was not an ounce of sympathy for me, just more of the harsh reality of life in the Workhouse. Well that's all done with now thank goodness."

I must say though that in view of how things developed with Jane I did wonder in later years if she had anything to do with Catherine taking her own life. I wondered if there had been any bullying going on that no one knew about. It was all a big, sad puzzle. Later, on a beautiful spring day, I walked through the meadows by the canal near the White Swan Inn and with the birds singing cheerfully and the fresh leaves on the trees it was hard to believe that it had been the scene of such a tragedy.

As expected I went into service when I was fourteen. The Matron of the Workhouse had called me to her office one day. There was a lady there called Mrs Pritchard who wanted a house servant. It was quite the usual thing for people who wanted servants to come to the workhouse to find a young girl. They knew that we were trained to do housework and laundry work. We were used to hard living.

"This is Mary, Mrs Pritchard. She's a hard worker and doesn't cause trouble. She'll make a good house servant for you. Now what do you say Mary?

"Yes ma'am." And then I had been trained to make a little bob curtsey, so I did and that very day went off with Mrs Pritchard to her house in Burcott Road.

Mrs Pritchard's husband was a stonemason and he had his yard at the back of the house. But his main work at that time and for many years was to be involved with the restoration of the Cathedral. On Easter Monday 1786 there had been a terrible disaster when the West Tower had collapsed taking with it the West Front and part of the nave. Over the ensuing years there was much rubble to be cleared and sorted for as much stone as possible would be used again. Plans had to be drawn up and a vast amount of money had to be raised before the restoration could begin over fifty years later.

Grandmother Ann who had been longing to see the Cathedral when she came from America was shocked by the ruin that met her eyes; unfortunately she never did have the chance to see the cathedral in all its glory as the restoration wasn't started until the year after she died and in fact the Cathedral did not open again until 1863 which was some years after I had moved away from Hereford.

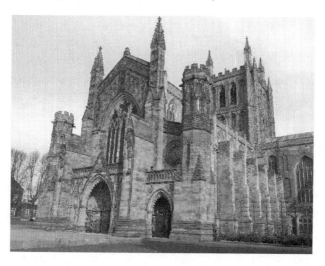

9. Hereford Cathedral

During the time I was a servant for the Pritchards the master went off most days to work in the temporary shelter that had been erected close by the Cathedral. Carving stone was such a skilled craft I realised, when a slip with the chisel could ruin hours and hours of work previously done. It was dangerous too for stones could fall and crush bones or even kill people. The master did some beautiful work which sometimes I was allowed to go and see. He was a very clever man and I realised that his work would be there for future generations to see long after our lives had finished. This was no wealthy household and Mrs Pritchard was no lady of leisure. While her husband was carving blocks of stone his wife was working as a laundress as well as minding her children who were very young and needed a lot of attention.

10. Present day masons' shelter, Hereford Cathedral

My work at the Pritchards was very hard. From early morning until late at night I was at their beck and call. I expected no particular kindness and I received none. My hands were raw from scrubbing floors, washing greasy dishes, making fires. My back ached from sweeping up dust and mess, of which there was plenty. In that house there was no peace. All was bustle and noise. No one cared about how I felt; I was just a skivvy. So you see what I mean when I said that when I left the workhouse it was not to a life of freedom but to a harsh life.

And in that harsh life there was very little time for pleasing myself. Whatever time I did have away from my work I spent at John's home or walking by myself near the River Wye or in the countryside that surrounded Hereford. I was not particularly unhappy although I sorely missed

Catherine and grieved over the way her life had ended but it was good to be free from the workhouse and I needed time to come to terms with the path my life had taken.

As I trod the country bye ways I puzzled over the inequalities in life; the poverty of some people; the life of ease of others. I realised that the tragedy of losing my parents when I was so young and of being thrust into the Workhouse where I spent my childhood had in fact given me the advantage of an education which many other poor people did not have. I resolved to build upon this advantage and to better myself whenever possible. I could not at the present time envisage how this could happen but I knew I must be open to any possible opportunity. There arose in me a small feeling of optimism, of determination that I would not sink under the blows of life but it wasn't long before another disaster loomed large. On my visits to John he had told me of his disquiet about Jane. "Mary she is keeping bad company. I have seen her around the town with a notorious character called James Probert. So watch out and my advice is to steer clear of her."

It wasn't long after that that I did indeed see her with this unsavoury looking character when we came upon each other in St Owen Street. "Oh if it isn't my baby sister," she crowed so loudly that people turned round to stare. "Look James, once seen, never forgotten. Let's go into the tavern and have a sup of beer and we can catch up."

She made me curl up inside but with my new mood of determination I wasn't going to let her intimidate me. James put his ugly hand on my shoulder and his face with its foul breath and rotten teeth came too close for comfort.

"Yes, good idea," he leered, looking me up and down suggestively, "then I can get to know your little sister."

"Not just now," I managed to say, "I'm on an errand for the mistress, another time."

"Please yourself then." Jane called after me as I walked away. That was a narrow escape I thought. Hopefully another time I'll see her coming and be able to slip out of the way. As it happened, it was only two or three months later in early October that I did catch a glimpse of her again when I saw her walking ahead of me in High Town. Either she had put on a lot of weight, I thought, or she was expecting but I didn't hang around to find out the truth of the matter.

"Oh yes she's living with that Probert fellow. Susannah Morgan out on the Ross Road takes in lodgers and they're living there. He's trouble in more ways than one. So now he's got her with child. Whatever next!" John said when I told him what I had seen. The next thing he told me was even more disquieting.

"I've heard he's also been using the name Joseph Williams and, as such, has a criminal conviction."

Things went from bad to worse and the next thing we heard was that she and this Probert fellow had been arrested for housebreaking. Their trial was fixed for 5th January 1853. When I next saw my sister Charlotte she already knew all about it. "The brazen hussy had it coming to her," was all she would say on the matter.

Mrs Pritchard kindly gave me time off to go to the trial as

long as I made up the work later. John didn't go to the brickworks either on that day even though he could well have done without the loss of a day's pay. I don't think supporting Jane was uppermost in our minds as there didn't seem to be much doubt of her guilt, but after all she was our sister and we wanted to know the truth of the matter. So we both went to the court.

I was shocked when she and Probert were led into the court room. It was some months since I had seen her briefly in High Town and she was by now very obviously heavily with child and looked unwell, dishevelled and cowed. By contrast Probert was full of himself, cocky, full of his own self-importance although no one else thought he was important at all. Mr Griffiths prosecuted the prisoners who were undefended.

They were charged with breaking into the home of Mrs Elizabeth Price at Burghill and stealing a woollen shawl valued at ten shillings, a silk dress valued at ten shillings, a woollen dress valued at five shillings and other articles which belonged to Elizabeth Price's daughter Catherine who was the first to give evidence.

"I live with my mother and we left our home on 20th October," she said. "In my bedroom on that day there was a box containing a silk dress, a mousseline de laine dress and a shawl. We returned home at about half past four and discovered to our horror that a hole had been made in the back wall of the house. We looked around and discovered that half a sovereign and some silver were missing in addition to the items already mentioned."

The wearing apparel was produced by Superintendent

Gregory and Catherine Price identified it as belonging to her. Next to give evidence was Edward Jones who was a lodger at Mrs Price's house.

"I lodge at Mrs Price's house and left a pair of boots there on that day. They were gone when I returned home."

Again Superintendent Gregory stepped forward and held up the boots.

"Aye, those are my boots." Edward Jones said.

James Lloyd, one of the constables of the parish of Burghill gave evidence that he had seen the prisoners near the house of Mrs Price in Burghill on the day of the robbery. Susannah Morgan was called next to give evidence. In reply to questioning she said,

"I keep a lodging house in Hereford and Jane Saint and James Probert were lodging there on 20th October. They left on that day not returning until Monday 4th November. P C Errington came to the house and wanted to know how many lodgers I had. He also wanted to see the prisoners bundle. I saw Jane Saint working at that silk dress trying to convert it into something else. She also showed me the shawl and asked me to pawn it for her. I did that and gave the money to Probert."

At this point Probert interrupted the proceedings and shouted out, "Who asked you to fetch the shawl downstairs for Errington to see?" Susannah Morgan replied,

"You did."

"If it hadn't been for you giving evidence I was going to plead guilty. And I'm going to warn you Susannah Morgan that though the pitcher might go often to the well it was sure to be broken at last and yours is cracked "

"Aye it is," she said, "but it was you who cracked it."

P C Errington said he had received the property from the last witness.

PC Gregory said he had received some of the property from Errington and some from Alfred Leach at Mr Myer's shop where he had apprehended Jane Saint when she had tried to pawn the dress. P C Gregory had previously left a sketch of the dress with him and a handbill with a description of the suspects.

Alfred Leach gave evidence: "When Jane Saint turned up at the shop and tried to pawn the dress I recognised her and sent for P C Gregory and she was caught."

Realising that the game was up Probert spoke up in a last ditch attempt to save Jane:

"This is all my fault not hers," he said. "I alone am guilty of the robbery. She is guiltless of the crime that has been imputed to her. I am totally to blame for having brought this present trouble upon her."

Then it was nearly all over. The learned Chairman summed up and after consulting briefly the jury found both prisoners guilty. A previous conviction was proved against Probert by James Jones, one of the turnkeys at the County Goal where he was indicted under the name of Joseph

Williams. He had also been convicted at the City Sessions. As Probert was sentenced to ten years transportation his cockiness returned:

"That's nothing when a fellow's used to it." was his only comment.

Jane was sentenced to twelve months imprisonment which she served in the gaol at Hereford but James Probert was transported to Australia, the other side of the world. Whether he ever came back or not I do not know.

Mr Griffiths applied for the expenses of Superintendent Gregory who took Mr Adams with him when he pursued the prisoner into Wales. Mr Adams went because he knew the prisoner and Gregory did not. The expenses of between £4 and £5 were allowed.

It was strange to think that only a few yards from John's house in Gaol Lane Jane was incarcerated in prison. It was there that her baby was born a few weeks later. She named him James. I thought at first she had named him after our Uncle James but then realised with a jolt she had named him after that criminal James Probert. So she had cared for him after all. By now he was probably in a convict ship in the Thames estuary awaiting transportation to Australia.

When she came out of prison she was a chastened woman; not for her the false bravado that James Probert had exhibited at his trial. She was back in the workhouse, being quite destitute. Further disappointment awaited her, for the baby sickened and died of bronchitis a month after her sentence ended.

11. Hereford Gaol

During 1853 changes were afoot in Hereford that would link it to the rest of the country and bring it finally into the modern world. A railway line had been constructed running south from Shrewsbury. During that year it had been open for freight traffic but on 6th December it was opened to passenger traffic as well.

For Charlotte, John and me a great cloud had hung over our lives since the tragic death of Catherine and Jane's shameful disgrace. The coming of the railway gave us the opportunity to change that and to start again away from the place where there had been so much hardship and unhappiness.

One October afternoon when the sun shone fitfully and the wind was stirring the leaves up in the gutters and whipping them round my legs I rapped at John's door and after calling out, "Anybody there?" I went in to their tiny parlour. It was Sunday so John was at home.

"I think we need to talk," he said to me, "so before you take your coat off come out with me for a walk and we'll have a chat."

We left his house in Gaol Lane and cut through a passageway into St Owen Street. Passing the Lamb Inn and the place where we had spent our early years we crossed over the road into Cantilupe Street. Where the road started to slope down towards the river children were throwing crusts to the ducks on the pond which was all that remained of the old castle moat. We went down the hill passing Castle Green on our right. The castle was long gone and on the green stood the memorial to Nelson.

John looked over to it and said,

"Did you know Mary there was supposed to be a statue of him on the top of it but money ran out so they just put an urn there instead?

"Oh money is always running out," I replied.

On we went down to the river where the path alongside it was not yet too muddy. There were few boats on it that day and the leaves were starting to fall from the trees. Golden drifts of them landed on the water and floated away down the river.

"Where will they end up I wonder?" I asked John as they drifted off.

"It's where we will end up that I want to talk to you about." John said as he stopped and looked at me. "I want to get out of Hereford. Too much unhappiness has gone on here I want to make a new start. Our parents died far too young, I lost my first wife, we've both lost Catherine and Jane has brought shame on us all. We need a new start and with this new railway we can get it. The line goes to Shrewsbury and then connects with Wolverhampton and Birmingham. Industry is booming in that part of the country. There are new jobs and new opportunities. I've been talking to Charlotte and she agrees with me. Will you join us? Will you come north to Staffordshire? There is a new life for us there."

While I thought his idea over we continued on to the old bridge over the river and stood there looking back at the town.

"Grandfather William and Grandmother Ann came over this bridge when they came from America to make a new life in Hereford. I've known this all my life and it will be strange to move away," I said.

"Yes and look how far they had come, half way across the world." John replied. "We'll be going less than a hundred miles. We've always got the choice of whether to come back or not if it doesn't work out."

"Yes John, you are right. Let's go. Let's grasp the opportunity that this railway gives us. Let's leave the past behind us and hope the future is brighter."

Part Two

On the Move

So that is what we did. John wasn't keen to have another winter tramping out to the brickfields at Holmer. He and Maryanne with John's daughter Eliza settled at Tipton near Dudley and John became a coal dealer keeping his carthorse in a stable not far from the house and a cart in his yard nearby. I lived with John and his family in Sheepwash Lane for a while and then became a live-in servant again, nearby at the home of an up and coming industrialist, as did Charlotte.

The name Sheepwash Lane told of an agricultural life that was fast disappearing from that part of Staffordshire. There were rich seams of coal and iron ore, industry was booming and the green fields were fast disappearing. Numerous coal pits were marked by the winding gear that stood at the head of the mine shafts and at night the glow of the blast furnaces could be seen for miles.

A number of canals went through the town and were heavily used by local industry for transporting goods as were the railways that increased their extent year by year. There was massive expansion in the coal and iron industries and the chimneys of local factories belched smoke into the air. Houses and factories were built side by side and everything became covered in the black dust that soon gave the area its name, 'The Black Country'.

A year after we moved to Tipton Charlotte married John Bishop, a labourer in an iron works, and they lived in nearby Wednesbury and raised a family there.

Thus it was that I met William Hall and fell for his skin-deep charm and fancy words. In 1859 I was married from John and Maryanne's home in Tipton.

Did I have any love for Will then? I may have done at first but it soon faded away. And it wasn't helped by his brutality to me on our wedding night. I was shocked by the way he treated me. There was no love in his attitude. He was only interested in his 'rights' as a married man. But I'd experienced much hardship already in my life and had already learned to 'shut up and put up' so that was that. I just got on with it all, as usual.

My learning to read during my childhood at the workhouse was useful, and I saw on our marriage certificate that Will had falsified his age and place of birth; I began to wonder if he had lied about other things too. Had he lied to get work perhaps? Had he lied to me? If not by that time, he certainly did later. When we were first married he was a labourer, probably almost illiterate if I remember rightly. I helped him to improve his reading and although I helped him better himself he didn't like me 'bossing him about' as he put it.

Our first three children William, James and Nimrod were born while we still lived in Staffordshire. I was getting fed up with the smoke and dirt and, fondly remembering the green fields of Herefordshire, I encouraged Will to apply for a job in the Worcestershire Police Force. "Will, just think, there will be a house with the job. You'll get uniform provided as well, so that will save money. You'll look so smart and people will think you are important," I pointed out.

These things all appealed to him, especially the idea of being able to swagger round the place poking his nose into other people's business and telling them what to do. So he was pleased when his application to join the Worcestershire Police Force in 1864 was successful. With our three small boys we were glad to have the house that went with the new job in the pretty village of Inkberrow with its half-timbered black and white buildings. It was wonderful to be back in the clean air again and away from all the noise and pollution. Susannah was born there in August 1866. We named her after my poor mother. I was happy there and, so far as I knew, William was behaving himself.

After a couple of years we moved again to another police house in the village of Clent, ten miles away from Birmingham and that was where John Thomas was born in 1868. We had chickens in the garden at the foot of the hills and the children had the freedom to roam the countryside. By September 1872 William had started getting into trouble. Impatient with the squabbling children at home and with the wet washing hanging inside to dry on rainy days he increasingly went down to the Bell and Cross for a pint or two, which usually turned into a whole evening of drinking. Many times he accused me of nagging, "Will, don't keep going down there. What will people think?"

"Oh there you go again. You watch it woman or I'll shut your mouth for you." He scowled as he raised a fist to me. Yes, he'd started to hit me. I began to be afraid to go out in case the bruises showed. But it got worse when he started drinking during the day as well. I'd see him staggering up the lane back to the cottage when he should have been on the beat. "Checking up on me are you, you slut?" He'd sneer if he saw me looking down the lane. His bosses warned him that if he continued to be drunk on duty he would be dismissed.

"What do you think the neighbours are saying when they see you like this? What sort of example are you setting to the farm hands?" He brought his face with its foul breath up close to me and grabbed my hair. I screamed as he pulled and twisted it and pushed me so roughly so that I landed on the edge of the kitchen range. He stood over me and shouted,

"I won't stand for any more of yer blathering yer bloody bitch. I'm off."

The terrified children heard all this, as Will took no care to keep his voice down and they gazed in horror from the doorway. As I struggled to get up I couldn't believe that my marriage had fallen to such a low ebb. Something had to be done. Finally he must have heeded the warnings because he chose to resign rather than be dismissed. When he came home and told me what he'd done I all but screamed at him,

"Now what are we going to do? We're going to be without a home and without any money coming in either. How do you think I'm going to feed five children, eh? You're the most irresponsible oaf I've ever seen."

He came at me then and I was really frightened but for some reason he turned away at the last minute. Perhaps he was beginning to see what his behaviour had brought us to. So we did what most impoverished people from rural areas did at that time, we made for Birmingham; for the streets full of people and carts; for the smoke and stink; for the back to back houses with whole families living crowded together in one or two rooms, houses that were gathered round a court with one tap for everyone and a line of shared water closets in the middle, where everyone knew everybody else's business, where everyone knew about the starvation and lack of food to put on the table, where a visit to the pawnshop during the week was followed by reclaiming your possessions if you had enough money at the end of the week on payday.

How far we had fallen from the open fields and leafy lanes of Worcestershire. It was so depressing. I had wanted so much more than this for my children. It was no better than where I had been born in the most unsanitary part of Hereford where filth and disease were commonplace. Will found a job sweeping factory floors. At least the long hours kept him from under my feet and brought some money in. Maybe those long hours gave him time to think and perhaps to realise how his actions had reduced us to this. One evening, in an uncharacteristically humble mood, he came to me,

"Mary," he said, "Look, I know this is all my fault. It's difficult for me to say this but I'm sorry I've brought all this upon you and the children and I'm going to find a way of putting things right again."

He'd realised that as he hadn't actually been sacked from the Worcester Police he could see if the Birmingham

Police Force would take him on. I thought they must be desperate if they would take on such a man as him and indeed they were. With the population going up with the influx of people flocking from rural areas for work, so the level of crime was going up too. After joining the Force in 1873 he seemed to have turned over a new leaf but only a year later things started to go downhill when he lost a day's pay as a result of being off his beat and spending twenty minutes in a water closet with a prostitute. How I got this information out of him I will never know. Can you blame me for rarely allowing him in my bed?

"You filthy specimen of humankind," I railed at him and he retorted,

"What's a man expected to do with a cold fish of a wife like you?"

He could be so hurtful.

Our daughter Mary was born in 1875 and was the last child we had.

Over the next twelve years the pattern became established when he was repeatedly fined for being away from his beat and being drunk on duty. The rows were constant. After all how was I expected to feed the family when he kept losing pay for his misdemeanours?

Finally matters came to a head when he was dismissed in 1887 for improper conduct with females. One of Will's fellow constables felt sorry for me and let me glimpse his police record. This was probably not allowed but it showed that his last set of crimes had included indecent behaviour to a female called Mary Jane Walker. She and her illegitimate child became inmates in Birmingham Workhouse, poor souls. What a dreadful start to a child's life. I knew only too well what they were going through.

However, by his usual smooth talking and smarmy ways he managed to get himself taken on as a night watchman in Birmingham's famous Jewellery Quarter and that is where we went to live next. At least that job kept him out of my bed at night not that he'd been in it much anyway. Can you blame me for my hatred of him?

Sadly the implications of William's dismissal had a far reaching effect on the life of our daughter Susannah as you will hear in the next chapter so I'll let her continue the story.

Chapter Five

Part One

Starting Out

In 1871 we were living in the little village of Clent in Worcestershire so I went with my brothers William, James and Nimrod to the village school. I was an able pupil and always enjoyed my lessons and when I was older I decided I wanted to be a teacher. Since the passing of the 1870 Education Act there had been an urgent need for teachers. All children now had to attend school so when I was thirteen I became a pupil teacher.

By this time we were living in Hockley in Birmingham where my father was a policeman. There had been the possibility that after five years of extra tuition I might have obtained a Queen's Scholarship and a place at one of the new Teacher Training Colleges but since I was hoping one day to get married and knew that as a married woman I would not be able to continue teaching, I decided to remain as a pupil teacher. And although my pay was very low I was able to give it to my mother to help with the housekeeping. All children were expected to do that when they started work.

As time went on I began to feel a degree of empathy with the children from poor homes because that had been my background too for many years when my father was being fined and losing pay for his misconduct. But many of the teachers at the school where I taught had no understanding of what it meant to be poor and troubled by violence at home. They looked with scorn at the children who had to come to school dirty and barefoot or who were wearing worn and patched clothes that had obviously been handed down from older siblings. Some of these children had eaten nothing before they came to school. And for them there was always the fear of being sent to the Workhouse hanging over their heads.

I would never forget what my mother had told me about her early years in the Workhouse in Hereford. My heart went out to those children. It was easy for them to let their concentration drift and then fall foul of a range of punishments from writing lines or wearing the dunce's hat to a beating with the cane.

At first I was a pupil teacher in the school at which I had been a pupil in Hockley but four years later I obtained a position as a pupil teacher at a school in Lozells, a very poor part of Birmingham. I no longer wished to live with my parents in Warstone Lane as the atmosphere at home was unbearable. There was constant rowing due to my father's unreliability as a policeman. Frequently he would be fined for not being on duty when he should have been or for being drunk on duty. He was also accused of immoral behaviour with a prostitute with whom he had spent twenty minutes in a water closet.

My poor mother had a lot to put up with, not least being the financial situation, as from one week to another she didn't know how much money she would get from my father for running the home and feeding the family. This was my opportunity to get out and to start to make my own life, so finding new lodgings became a matter of some urgency. This meant that my mother would have one less mouth to feed but she would nevertheless miss my contribution to the household purse although after paying for my food and lodging I did sometimes manage to give her a little money.

One sunny morning at the beginning of September as I was walking past a row of shops near the school I glanced in the window of a haberdashers and saw an advertisement from 'A respectable lady' offering lodgings to a single professional woman. "That's just what I'm looking for," I said to myself and, carefully making a note of the address which was about a mile away on Birchfield Road, I immediately set off to see if the room was still available and further more if I would find the landlady agreeable.

The house, with a small front garden, was on the road leading from Birmingham to Walsall so even in the 1880s it was quite busy. As I knocked at the front door I noticed the doorstep was neat and clean and that the net curtains at the front window were freshly laundered. I heard footsteps approaching the door, which was opened by a tall, slim lady, aged about fifty who was wearing a black dress and spectacles. Her greying hair was pulled tidily back into a bun, well secured by numerous hairpins.

"Good morning," she said, "what can I do for you?"

"Good morning," I replied, "My name is Miss Hall and I've come to see about the room you are advertising."

"Come in Miss Hall and we will have a talk about what

your requirements are then I will show you the room. My name is Miss Smith."

I went into the narrow hall and Miss Smith opened a door, which led into the front room where there was an aroma of lavender polish but also a faint air of a room not in frequent use. An embroidered fire screen stood in front of the tiled fireplace and a clock ticked quietly on the mantelpiece. In the small bay window behind the sofa a polished table protected by a lace mat displayed a maidenhair fern. Against the wall opposite the fireplace stood a rosewood piano its lid lifted to show the ivory keys and a sheet of music invitingly waiting to be played. On the top of the piano were displayed two photographs.

"My parents," Miss Smith volunteered when she saw where my glance fell.

We smiled at each other and she asked me if I would be working in the local area. I told her I would be teaching at a school a mile away in Lozells and I would require breakfast before I went to school and a meal in the evening. At the weekends I would also need a midday meal unless I was out visiting family. If possible I would need a table in my bedroom where I would be able to prepare my lessons. After she had told me what her charges were she said,

"I can arrange all that for you, but you'd better come and see if the room I have is acceptable to you."

She led me up the first flight of stairs explaining that a further flight led up to the attic where the maid of all work slept. We turned onto a landing where she opened the second door we came to. The room faced south and was flooded with sunshine from the window which offered a view of the pretty garden and the houses beyond. A small iron bedstead covered with a blue and white quilt had been placed to one side of the room; above the bed was an embroidered plaque with a message announcing that 'Cleanliness is next to Godliness.' There was a blue and yellow rag rug to step onto when you got out of bed to avoid putting your feet onto the varnished pine floorboards. Next to the bed was a marble topped washstand on which stood a bowl and ewer, and on the other side of the room stood a heavy oak wardrobe; near the window was an armchair with a patchwork cushion.

"This is the room," Miss Smith said," but as you can see at the moment it does not have a work table in it but I'm sure we can find one somewhere; and you'll need a chair to sit at when you are working."

"It's a lovely room," I said, "and if you are happy for me to live here I would like to take the room." I felt that Miss Smith and I would get on well. And that proved to be the case.

She had lived in this house for many years with her parents, caring for them as they aged; she had never married. The photograph of her parents on top of the piano in the parlour showed her father as a rather forbidding gentleman but maybe he was asked to take that pose by the photographer. After he died she had lived there with her mother while their financial resources dwindled alarmingly. Her mother's recent death and the need to supplement her meagre income had prompted the idea of taking in a lodger.

I lived with Florence Smith for several years and got to know her well. She became a good friend. As an only child of strict non-conformist parents she had a well-developed sense of social justice, especially regarding the children of the poor and those abandoned by their parents. After both of her parents had died she moved away from the narrow non-conformity of her childhood. So with her I sometimes attended Carr's Lane Congregational Church in Birmingham town centre and was inspired by the preaching of Dr Dale. Often the pews on the ground floor were full by the time we arrived so with many other worshippers we would climb the stairs to the gallery that swept round three sides of the church. From there we had a good view of the pulpit situated in the centre at the front of the church with the magnificent organ behind it. Unlike the Anglican churches I had been used to this church had no altar and thus no altar rail and during the Communion services the twelve deacons distributed the bread and wine to the members of the congregation who remained seated in alternate pews.

Dr Dale was a very famous preacher and was the Minister of Carr's Lane Church for forty years. We found his sermons stimulating and they gave us much food for thought and discussion regarding social reform and the fundamental causes of poverty and crime. He was especially interested in preaching the 'Civic Gospel' an idea which had been promoted by another well-known preacher of the time, George Dawson, who had died a few years previously.

12. Carrs Lane interior
Photo: Frank Williams

On my return from school I would frequently find a tea tray laid for two on which were hot buttered pikelets under a silver cover.

"Come and sit down and tell me how it went today," Florence would say as she poured the tea.

"I'm beginning to settle in," I replied, "but it worries me that some of those little mites are half-starved and with winter coming on I know they are going to be so cold in those rags they wear. The Evans children didn't turn up today. I heard the family has been taken into the workhouse so that means the parents will be split up and the children will be separated from them as well."

"Yes Susannah it's a sad state of affairs. But thank goodness there is some improvement nowadays because many of these children can live in smaller groups of about thirty in the cottage homes that are being built like the ones at Moseley. They are well cared for in a clean environment and receive good food and have house parents to look after them rather than the workhouse staff."

"I am reminded of Lord Shaftsbury's view that the future hopes for the country lie with the children, not with the adults. For them it is too late and as he remarked 'As the sapling has been bent so it will grow'," I added.

"We have seen many improvements in social conditions in the last fifty years particularly regarding the laws relating to the employment of children and their education but there is still a very long way to go." Florence said.

One day she had a surprise for me when I got home on Friday evening. "Tomorrow night we're going to a concert in the Town Hall," she said. "I have tickets for a programme of music by Handel, Mozart and Schubert."

"What a treat that will be," I replied with some excitement, "I shall look forward to it so much."

So the following evening we travelled into town and decided to walk around to the back of the Town Hall before the concert started to see the memorial that had been erected in 1880 to commemorate the public service of Joseph Chamberlain. It had been placed to the front of the Art Gallery that was currently under construction. Of course we had been to see it before but it was always a pleasure to admire again its neo-gothic style and appreciate how the layout of the town had improved in the last twenty to thirty years, thanks very largely to the man whose vision it celebrated.

We joined the queues of people waiting for admittance to the Town Hall. I had only been there on one or two previous occasions and was always impressed by its classical style of architecture outside and by its magnificence within. There was seating on the ground floor and also on two balconies. The lower one stretched along the back and part of the way round two sides of the building and from the higher one, where we sat on the cheaper seats; a splendid view was spread out beneath us. However the gas lighting used in the building not only produced a rather smoky, yellow light but a great deal of heat which often caused a number of people in the upper gallery to faint.

The concertgoers in bright clothes chatted animatedly while we all waited for the entrance of the conductor. On a raised platform the orchestra finished tuning their instruments. Behind them was the splendid pipe organ that had cost £6,000 when it was installed in the newly built Town Hall in 1834. As soon as the leader of the orchestra tapped his music stand an expectant hush fell over the audience and, as the members of the orchestra stood to welcome the conductor, the audience rendered polite applause.

"Isn't this exciting?" Florence whispered. I nodded my head in agreement as I smiled back at her. There followed two hours of exquisite music when all the cares of the trivial round and daily task melted away. As we came away afterwards and walked along Paradise Street I felt so happy. I had enjoyed the music immensely.

Such treats as that were rare, but when I could spare the time from my lesson preparation I often ventured into town on Saturday afternoons to admire the new buildings and enjoy the shops. Everywhere was busy with the bustle and noise of people and the carriages and horse drawn trams that rattled up and down the streets. I felt sorry for the two horses that had to pull such a heavy load and you had to be very careful not to put your foot in their dung when crossing the road. Street cleaners were constantly clearing it away.

One of my favourite places to visit when it opened in 1885 was the Museum and Art Gallery just round the corner from the Council House and opposite the Chamberlain Memorial. The opening of this building had a been a rather interesting example of Industry literally supporting Art as the Gas Committee had their offices on the ground floor. The lofty proportions of the entrance and staircase leading up to the galleries were impressive and the peace and quiet of the rooms with their high ceilings brought a welcome relief from the tensions I experienced in overcrowded classrooms. The displays of paintings, sculpture and works of art were enthralling and I often went in to admire them standing in front of a painting for as much as ten minutes to absorb fully its beauty and meaning.

Sometimes I noticed a tall, fair-haired young man who was already on the train when I went into town at the weekend. He began to notice me too and raised his hat when we left the train together at New Street Station. I saw him at the Art Gallery on more than one occasion and also noticed that from time to time he was in the audience at the Town hall concerts. I thought it would be nice to know a little more about him, but shyness prevented me from making the first move.

And then one winter several weeks went by when I didn't see him at all. I thought he must have moved away from the area. However at the end of February 1886 he reappeared and one Saturday morning as we left the train together he spoke to me. "Good morning," he said, raising his hat to me, "I've missed seeing you. I think we should introduce ourselves, I'm Evan Voice."

"I've also missed seeing you, I'm Susannah Hall, I teach in Lozells."

"And I'm a jeweller. Will you come and have a coffee with me? It's such a cold morning that it will be good to get inside and into a warm place."

And so began our friendship, which gradually developed into courtship and eventually into marriage but I move on too fast.

On another occasion when we met I told him that although my family now lived in the town I had been born in the countryside in the village of Inkberrow in Worcestershire and later lived in Clent.

"My family also used to live in the country," he told me. "We lived in the small village of Castle Bromwich in Warwickshire about six miles from Birmingham. So why did you leave Worcestershire?"

"Oh it was because my father was looking for work," I replied.

"It was for the same reason that we came to live in the town" he told me. "My father was born and bred in Castle Bromwich where his ancestors had lived for generations and after my parents were married they lived in a tiny cottage there. As the family grew the tiny cottage was bursting at the seams. Birmingham was also growing and my father reckoned that he could continue his work as a coachman and gardener and live in a better house. So we moved into Birmingham about fifteen years ago. He soon found a job working for one of the wealthy industrialists who had moved in to the pleasant area of Handsworth Wood."

"Did your mother come from that village as well?"

"Oh no, she came all the way from Wales to find work in the town soon after her father died. And now I have two brothers and three sisters. One large happy family," he added with a smile, "Well, most of the time anyway. One of my sisters, Tilly, has already left home and is now a housemaid in Cheshire."

"I'm afraid my family life has not been as happy as yours. My poor mother had a very difficult time both in her early years and later in her marriage." But I couldn't bear to tell him how bad it really was. At that time I didn't know that the following year the effect of my father's notorious past would catch up with me and that I would have to be telling Evan all about my family life.

He gave me such a kind, sympathetic look and said, "We must make sure you are happy now. Do you play the piano and sing?"

"Yes," I answered, "I love music."

"Well then, one Sunday you must come to tea and share in one of our musical evenings. We love to gather round the piano and sing. My mother, being Welsh, has a beautiful voice and being half Welsh myself maybe I've inherited some of it but I'll leave you to judge for yourself about my singing capabilities," he said with a grin. "Unfortunately I'm prone to coughs so I sometimes run out of breath."

That was something to really look forward to and after thanking Evan for the coffee and giving him my address so that he would be able to contact me, we parted, I to buy some gloves and he to look for some sheet music for his mother.

It was only a few days later that I received a note from him in the post. I had already told Florence that I'd spoken to the young man I had seen from time to time and that a few days earlier we'd had coffee together. She was nearly as excited as I was when his note arrived. I think she saw a budding romance but I chided her that it was too soon to think of that. "I shall keep my hopes to myself then but you just wait and see, my girl!"

So the following Sunday afternoon Evan arrived to escort me to his home. I introduced him to Florence and they chatted while I fetched my hat, coat and gloves. Afterwards she told me she thought he was a 'very nice young man' and gave me a knowing look.

Although it was only the last day of February the sun was shining and we enjoyed the walk through the quiet, almost rural roads to his house in Wellington Road. When we arrived there was an excited hum of chatter from inside the house and I was introduced to everybody. His mother and father were there and his brothers Thomas and young Harry, and also sisters, Lizzie and Alice. Immediately I noticed how different Evan and Thomas were. Evan was tall and fair and Thomas was not as tall and was more rounded and his hair was darker.

I found it rather overwhelming being with all of them that first time but I needn't have worried. Nobody was out to embarrass me by making me play the piano or sing on my own. Everyone was there just to have fun and enjoy the music and the company.

As Evan's mother was Welsh they had decided to celebrate St David's Day a day early as everyone would be back at work the next day. So a large vase of early daffodils was on a side table and Evan's father, proud of his gardening prowess, had put a few leeks in the vase as well. When my puzzlement about the inclusion of the leeks could be seen on my face Evan's Mam said,

"You may not know Susannah but daffodils and leeks are our national emblems which we enjoy displaying on the day of the patron saint of Wales."

"Ah, now I understand," I said.

"They do smell a bit of onions though. Not sure that's right in a vase of flowers," said Evan's Pa as he gave me a cheeky smile and scratched his head.

We all gathered round the piano and Evan's mother was the first to accompany us that evening. She sang some of her favourite Welsh songs that she had known since childhood; 'Land of my Fathers' and 'David of the White Rock' were two I remember from that evening. Then we sang some English folk songs and some favourites from our own time.

After about an hour Evan took over at the piano and his mother and Lizzie disappeared into the kitchen to finish preparing supper. We had cold meat, salad leaves from the garden, freshly made bread and pickles. It was delicious. They all made me so welcome; there was such a spirit of warm friendliness about them all, something that had been sadly lacking in my own home.

The following months had more of these happy occasions and eventually I became confident enough to play the piano. I loved those evenings, which continued right through the summer and following winter.

Sometimes Evan and I would go on our own to concerts at the Town Hall or to see exhibitions at the Art Gallery or just to walk in Handsworth in what was still at that time an almost rural area. Florence was right after all, romance was in the air. But early in March in 1887 my life was to go sadly wrong as my chosen work as a teacher came to an abrupt end.

I had been teaching for about four very satisfying years when, one Friday afternoon the headmaster, Mr Davenport, called me into his office. The school bell had rung for the end of lessons and the children had streamed across the schoolyard and out of the gate. I tapped on his door nervously wondering what I had done wrong.

"Come in Miss Hall," As I stood facing him across his desk he said, "Something very disturbing has come to my notice but first I want to be sure of my facts so I have a few questions for you."

My legs were trembling by now and I hoped he was going to ask me to sit down but he did not.

"Firstly, are you the daughter of William Hall?"

"Yes sir," I answered wondering what was coming next about the black sheep in our family.

"And am I right in thinking that he was recently dismissed from the Birmingham Police Force for gross misconduct?"

"Yes sir," more timidly.

"Well I'm afraid Miss Hall that puts me in a very difficult position. I have no alternative than to be decisive in this matter and I have to tell you that your employment in this school and any other in this area cannot be tolerated any longer. We cannot appear to condone that man's actions by employing a member of his family to teach here. We can only have people teaching here whose credentials are blameless. Although you may feel, and with some justification I am sure, that this dismissal comes through no fault of yours nevertheless a dismissal it has to be and with immediate effect. Please clear your belongings from your desk and classroom cupboards and leave this afternoon." And he returned his gaze to the more important matters that were awaiting him on his desk.

I couldn't believe my ears and was too shocked to make

any answer other than a muttered,

"Yes sir."

"Good afternoon, Miss Hall."

I walked away from his office in a daze and went back to my classroom; but it was no longer mine I realized sadly. I looked around at the rows of desks and messy inkwells, at the basket holdings the girls' sewing efforts, at the charts of tables and spellings hanging on the wall, at the large globe on top of the cupboard and the cane, which I never used, lying on the teacher's desk. I would be leaving all this behind me.

Furthermore I would miss the children so much, the naughty ones as well as the good children. In fact maybe I would miss the naughty ones more as I knew that many of them had a dreadful home life and had hoped that I could offer them some kindness and understanding. At this point I looked up at the ceiling where naughty Frank Williams had aimed a compass so well that it had stuck there seemingly for ever. That boy only survived in the school because he was a brilliant pianist and played jaunty tunes as the children marched out of assembly.

I packed up the books of my own that I had used and found a strong bag to put them in; I put on my coat and hat and closing the classroom door behind me for the last time, crossed the school hall with its polished wooden floor. I went along a short corridor and out into the school yard where at the beginning of morning and afternoon lessons the boys lined up at one door and the girls at another when the monitor rang the school bell. Then I went through the school gate and into the street and there, that was it. That was the end of my time as a teacher.

I couldn't believe this was happening to me. That something I had wanted to do for so long and had been doing successfully, had all come to an end because of my ghastly father. Now the shock was leading to anger. And that anger had to be vented on the person who deserved it, my father.

He and my mother were living in Warstone Lane and it was in that direction my feet were taking me as fast as possible. So on I marched from the school in Lozells, back to my lodgings to deposit my heavy bag and leave a note for Florence to say I would be back later and would not need a meal. Then I began my long walk through Hockley, into Great Hampton Street and into the Jewellery Quarter where all the jewellers had their tiny workshops. These were often crammed into what had been the gardens of the larger houses that fronted onto the street. I realised that it was somewhere in this area that Evan came every day to work as a jeweller mounter.

I turned from Vyse Street into Warstone Lane and despite my preoccupation with the misfortune that had befallen me, noticed the bright daffodils nodding their heads cheerfully in the cemetery alongside the road. When I arrived at my parents' house I banged on the door and went straight in. My mother, who was starting to get a meal ready, looked up in surprise.

"Where is he?" I glared at my mother and my twelve-year-old sister Mary.

"Susannah, whatever is the matter?" my mother asked with alarm.

"I'll tell you what the matter is. My wretched father has just lost me my job. Teaching was all I ever wanted to do and now because of his reputation as a drunkard and womaniser and his dismissal from the Police Force I am no longer fit to teach it seems. I am no longer wanted. They seem to think I might be tarred with the same brush."

My sister looked on in horror as, with my anger suddenly spent, I subsided onto a chair by the table and dissolved into floods of tears.

"I'll put the kettle on," she said while my mother came over and put an arm round my shoulders.

"Now take your coat off love and we'll have a nice cup of tea." She took my coat and hung it up on a peg behind the door, "I just don't know what to say to comfort you. Now tell me what happened?"

I told her what had gone on after school that afternoon and she agreed with me that it was all most dreadfully unfair.

"But that's your father all over, love. Throughout my marriage to him he's been nothing but trouble. Quite honestly ranting and raving at him won't bring your job back and won't do you any good. Have a cup of tea with us and then go back to your lodgings and we'll all have a think about what is to be done now. And don't you worry anymore about handing over any money to me. Without a job you just won't be able to, so that's that. "

I knew she was right and so decided not to stay and confront him. Just as she had done over the years I had to pull myself together and make the best of things. I realised that for her too my dismissal had come as a great disappointment. With the hardship of her early years behind her she had so desperately wanted her family to rise above the poverty and lack of culture of those years. So still angry about the injustice of it all I left them when I had finished my tea and made my way back along Vyse Street.

It was a chilly evening and I turned my collar up. Although unhappy and deep in thought about what I was going to do next I became aware of footsteps hurrying after me.

"Susannah, is that really you?" I turned and saw Evan quickly coming along the street behind me. He was quite out of breath when he caught up with me and by the time he had caught his breath again he had noticed my eyes were red from crying. "My dear girl, whatever is the matter?" He put an arm round my shoulders and looked so concerned that he almost set me off crying again.

"Evan I've lost my job."

"Why? Whatever has happened?"

"Oh, Evan, I knew I would have to tell you about my dreadful father sometime, it's really terrible." And so I recounted the events of the afternoon to him. "They've decided, that coming from such a disreputable family I must be like that too, so I'm no longer wanted."

Now I could no longer hold back the tears and Evan drew me to him and whispered words of endearment while my tears rolled down the front of his coat. "Now come along, we can't have you standing here crying on street corners. Here's a handkerchief for you, dry your eyes, come with me and we'll go home and see what suggestions Mam has to make about this."

"Oh Evan I can't do that. Whatever will your mother think of me?"

"She'll love you even more, don't you worry and she'll have a plan of action in next to no time. Come along, dry your eyes, tuck your arm into mine and off we go."

So that is what we did and Evan's mother, dear that she is, rubbed the flour off her hands with her apron and put her arms round me when she heard the sad story. Then she carried on making the spotted dick pudding and said, "Don't you worry my duck, we'll soon sort something out. We're just going to have a bite to eat and then we'll think of something." As usual the 'bites to eat' in the Voice household were substantial and tasty although that evening I was not able to do the meal justice.

What a lovely happy family they were. Evan's father, Charley, had a very productive garden that helped to feed the family. Thomas, four years younger than Evan, was also a jeweller and he was courting Annie by then. I soon came to know Annie and we became close friends. Then there was Evan's much younger brother Harry, quite a handful, as I would find out before long. Alice was twelve at that time and would soon be leaving school. With her ability for fine sewing she was destined to be a dressmaker.

116

Then there was Lizzie, fifteen and already working as a laundress.

"Susannah," she said as she leant across the table, "You've no idea what all that water and steam does to a girl's hands and hair."

"Oh you're so vain Lizzie." Alice chipped in and, with her nose in the air and a mischievous look on her face, added, "She's after the boys Susannah. Don't you think she's too young?"

"Now don't involve Susannah in your banter," Evan's Mam said with a stern look. "She's got enough worries of her own."

"Oh Susannah," Lizzie said, "Whatever has happened to you?"

And it all came out in front of everyone, which wasn't necessarily what I would have chosen, but maybe that was for the best. The result was that the whole family was on my side and applying themselves to finding a solution to my employment problem.

"Well there is factory work." Lizzie said.

"No," Evan said, "that's not suitable."

"Or a domestic servant of some kind." suggested his mother, "Yes, maybe something like that would be the best thing."

"Now who do we know that needs a housemaid? Let's all have a good think about this." Lizzie added.

"Susannah, I'm a coachman and hear a lot about the well-to-do folk around here. I'll keep my ears open and put in a good word for you. I'm sure something will come up soon." Evan's Pa said with a concerned look on his face.

"You're all very kind, I'm already feeling more optimistic. So on that positive note I think it's time I went back to my landlady. She'll be wondering where I have got to."

"And in the meantime," Evan's father put in," Don't forget that our great Queen, is coming to visit Birmingham next week."

"I know she's on her Jubilee Tour but is she coming to Birmingham for any particular reason?" Evan's Mam asked.

"Yes," said Thomas, "She's coming to lay the Foundation Stone for the New Law Courts for which a site has been found beyond Old Square on Corporation Street."

"I haven't been shopping in town for a while because I can get all I need here in Handsworth so let's go in to see the Queen and make it an opportunity to see the new shops at the same time." Evan's Mam said enthusiastically. "It's all been changing so much in that part of town in the last few years."

"I hear a lot of shop owners in New Street and the High Street are not happy about losing their trade to those new shops on Corporation Street," Evan added thoughtfully.

"Neither are the people who lived in the slums that have been demolished to make way for that new road." Thomas added, "They have lost their homes and no new ones are being built for them."

"So whose idea was it then to do all this knocking down and building up again?" Alice asked.

"Joseph Chamberlain has been the mover behind this scheme and many of the others that have affected this town in the last twenty years. He's moving with the times and wants Birmingham to be a great city. Look at the industry that has come here in the last hundred years or so, look at the impressive new buildings we have like the Art Gallery and the Council House; look at the new lighting, water supplies and sewerage that have been put in. You can't have an eyesore and health risk like the slums that were in the Upper Priory, the Gullet and the Minories in a modern, forward looking city can you?" Evan explained.

"Certainly not," Charley added, "Just think how glad we were to move in from Castle Bromwich to a better house with a water closet that wasn't at the end of the garden path and with a cold tap actually inside the kitchen rather than a pump outside that we shared with four other cottages."

Harry was getting restless with this conversation that he didn't really understand, so tugging at his father's sleeve, he asked,

"Can we go and see her Pa?"

"Ah yes, back to the Queen's visit. It's a Wednesday so some of us have to be at work." replied Evan. "Have you got the day off school Harry? And you too Alice?"

"Yes I think we have," said Alice.

Evan's Mam turned to me and said,

"What about you, Susannah, would you like to go into town to see the Queen?"

"Yes I would," I replied.

"Well count me in," she said tapping a finger for each person added to the group, "and so that's Harry, Alice, and Susannah.

"And I might bump into you in town as I expect I'll be taking a carriage load of people." Evan's Pa said.

Evan got up and fetched my coat and waited patiently while his Mam gave me a hug.

"Don't worry my dear," she said in her lovely lilting Welsh voice, "we'll soon sort something out for you."

"Come on, Susannah, I'm walking you back home."

"Everyone in your family is so kind to me. I don't know what I've done to deserve this."

"We all love you, especially me," he said with a grin. He had made me blush again.

As we walked through the darkening streets to my lodgings on Birchfields Road Evan tucked my arm into his and we walked along cosily together and I began to feel safe and protected. We arrived on Florence's doorstep and I realised I was just about to have to go through the whole story again but she had become a good friend and I knew that she too would do all she could to help me.

As I began to get the key out of my purse the door opened and there she was.

"Good evening Evan. I thought I heard your voices and having been anxious about you Susannah I wanted to see you as soon as possible. Are you coming in Evan?"

"No thank you Miss Smith, I must get back. Goodnight Susannah. I'll come for you on Sunday afternoon as usual but of course you have your trip to see the Queen before that haven't you?" And with that he raised his hat to us both and saying, "Good night ladies," he turned and went back down the garden path, out through the gate and walked briskly down the road.

"Now Susannah come in and tell me what has been happening to you today. While you take your coat off I'll be putting the kettle on."

I began to realise how lucky I was not only to have Evan and his family being concerned for me but here was Florence too. We sat down by the fire and while she poured in the milk and then the tea I told her about the shock I had had when Mr Davenport called me into his office and dismissed me from my job.

"Susannah that's insane," she said, "Here are you, having been a good and reliable teacher there for, how long is it? About four years? And all of a sudden the notoriety of your father looms over you like a monster and you lose your job because of it."

"Well, Florence you are right he is a monster. He's a monster my poor mother has had to live with all these years and now he's sitting on my shoulder too. I just don't know what will happen. Obviously teaching is not an option now at all."

"Do you have any ideas about what you are going to do?"

"Well no, not really. I haven't had much time to think about the future."

"The trouble is that there are not very many opportunities open to an intelligent woman like you, other than teaching. I assume that for you factory work is out of the question?"

"Well, I hope not to do that but I have to earn my living so I may have to go into service."

"Yes, a possibility is to be a housemaid in one of the wealthier households here in the town. What do you think about that?"

"It sounds better than factory work, but don't you think I might be up against the same problem there, that once my father's character and disgrace are known it will be 'no thank you, we don't want your sort here.'? I just feel so despondent about the whole thing. I had so much hoped to rise above my background. It seems to me we are in a society that doesn't recognise you for your own worth but labels you according to what your parents, and in this case, father, have done with their lives."

"Yes it's rather the reverse of boys getting on in the world because they went to the right Public School or because their fathers are successful in business. It's not a fair world. People should be judged on their own merits. And of course, as women, we are hampered even more being supposedly the weaker sex. Pah, what nonsense. And even at universities although women are allowed to attend lectures and can even qualify for first class honours these days, they still cannot actually be awarded degrees. It's certainly not a fair world for women. Anyway, look Susannah, we could go on like this for ages, but I think we need a good night's sleep to decide what the best course of action is. But first of all tell me about the plans for your visit to see the Queen."

And so after I had told her what we were hoping to do the discussion for that evening ended but I could not settle properly to a good night's sleep as the events of the day were all too vivid in my mind.

****

Part Two

A Royal Visit

Of course there was no miraculous job waiting for me in the morning or indeed for several weeks. Florence, dear lady that she was, wouldn't accept a penny in rent from me while I wasn't earning so I determined to help her in as many ways as I could. She was getting older and was not as strong as when I first went to live with her so I determined to help with the cooking and any other jobs she needed doing. And in the few weeks that I remained living with her I was able to do that.

So on Wednesday 23rd March I met Evan's Mam, Alice and Harry at Perry Bar station near the end of Wellington Road. Harry and Alice were very excited about going for a ride on a train as it didn't happen very often.

While we stood waiting on the neat platform with its attractive beds of daffodils planted and cared for by the stationmaster, Harry was too excited to stand still and kept walking around looking at the other people who were waiting and peering up the track in the direction the train would come from. His Mam said, "When the train comes I'm going to hold on to you young man. I don't want you falling underneath it." Finally in the distance we could hear the chug, chug, chug of the train and as it came round the bend we could see the smoke from the funnel billowing into the sky.

"Ooh, here it comes." Harry cried, "Isn't it huge and noisy?" Alice covered her ears and took a step back. Clearly she found the noise a bit overwhelming.

Just before it came into the station the train's whistle screeched and the enormous black, clanking monster slowly came to a stop in front of us belching out smoke. It towered above us and when suddenly steam hissed out from around the wheels, Alice let out a shriek.

"All aboard. Hurry along please." The stationmaster shouted.

We found a second class compartment with only three people in it so there was room for us. It seemed the whole world was going into Birmingham to see the Queen. Three more people piled in behind us so we had to squash up and Harry was disgruntled at having to sit on his mother's knee. He tried to peer out of the open window.

"Pull that window up at once Harry or we'll get covered in smuts from the smoke." His Mam said sternly.

The guard went along the platform holding his green flag and slamming any doors that were still open.

"Where's the guard going?" Harry wanted to know.

"Oh Harry, everybody knows that he waves his flag when he gets to the end of the train to let the driver know it's safe to go." Alice replied sarcastically. "Then he jumps in the guards' van as the train sets off, clickety clack along the rails"

"Now miss, don't be so superior," her mother admonished

"You don't know everything either you know."

Harry nonchalantly peered out of the windows and announced each station as we came to it,

"Witton, Aston, Duddeston." And at last, "New Street, here we are!"

People poured out of the compartments and made their way along the platform.

"Tickets please!" Called the ticket collector at the end of the platform, so we handed them over and were soon leaving the station and emerging into Stephenson's Place.

Evan's Mam looked at Alice and wetting the corner of a hankie with a bit of spit pulled Alice to her and removed a smut from her face.

"We can't have smuts spoiling your beauty can we my love?" Then turning to me she continued, "Susannah where do you think the best place will be to see the Queen?"

"I'm thinking that somewhere near the Town Hall and Council House would be just right." I replied.

"Good. Let's make our way up there then."

We joined the happy, laughing crowds that jostled each other in New Street and slowly made our way up to a position near Christ Church at the top. The place was thronged with crowds, and street hawkers moved up and down selling Union Jack flags. There also hot potatoes, toffee apples, sweets, and pictures of the Queen being sold. Everybody was smiling, chattering excitedly and enjoying their day out.

We'd heard that Her Majesty would be visiting the Town Hall and then having lunch in the Council House so I felt that from the steps of Christ Church we would have a good view of both places. Later on she would set off in her carriage along New Street and Corporation Street before laying the Foundation Stone of the new Law Courts.

The scene was impressive and there was such a wonderful atmosphere among all the people who had come to see their Queen Empress. For so many years since her beloved Albert's death over twenty-five years earlier she had shunned public appearances but now here she was in Birmingham on her Jubilee Tour and people were so glad to see her at last.

In the distance we could hear cheering and knew that she was on her way and that we would see her in a few minutes. There was much good-natured jostling for position among the crowds and people pushed the children to the front so that they would have a good view. As the Queen's carriage arrived in front of us a sea of flags erupted in a frenzy of waving and all around people were shouting,

"Hurrah! Hurrah! Long live the Queen!"

"Isn't she tiny?" Evan's Mam said to me as the small black clad figure of Her Majesty stepped down from her carriage.

"Who is the lady with her?" Alice asked.

"It's Princess Henry of Battenburg," I was able to tell her. "She is the Queen's youngest child, Princess Beatrice, and has been married to Prince Henry for two years. Apparently the Queen only allowed her to marry if the couple promised to live with her."

"Well she is the Queen so I suppose she can make whatever rules she likes." Alice replied.

After a short while the Queen appeared, waving regally, on the balcony of the Council House and again the crowds burst into ecstatic cheering until she turned away and went back inside.

"I'm so glad to be here. I shall remember this day for the rest of my life." Alice sighed contentedly.

"Me too," Harry added, "but I'm hungry and there's a lovely smell of baked potatoes coming from somewhere."

"Yes I'm getting peckish too," his mother joined in, "and what you can smell Harry is certainly baked potatoes and they are being sold by that man over there. Can you see his black oven on wheels? Let's go and have a look."

Now that the Queen had disappeared to have her lunch we decided we would all buy a hot potato and wander round looking at the shops before making our way to the end of Corporation Street for the stone laying ceremony. The hot potato man was doing a roaring trade. "Look Mam, he's got a sort of drawer with the fire in and then the oven is on top and right on the top is a chimney. And he can wheel it all around." Just then the man opened the firebox drawer and a shower of sparks shot out when he put in some more coal. He looked in the oven, prodded the potatoes and decided they were cooked and ready to sell. Each potato went into a folded piece of newspaper with a knob of butter and a pinch of salt. We handed over our money and sat on the church steps to eat our feast.

"Delicious." Alice pronounced licking the butter off her fingers.

"Was that good Harry?" I asked him.

"You bet it was," he said wiping his mouth with his sleeve.

We had already walked up New Street so we decided to go along Colmore Row, past St Philip's Church and across the churchyard and then into the far end of Corporation St to get to Old Square.

"Cor, look at that!" Harry exclaimed as we approached the place where the new law courts would be built. A pavilion of brightly coloured material had been constructed to shelter the Queen as she stood on a dais to perform the ceremony.

"That's very pretty," said Alice, "It will look good against the black clothes she's wearing." In front of the pavilion was a large stone supported on blocks of wood. At that moment there came a familiar voice behind us,

"Hello me ducks," and there was Evan's Pa grinning from ear to ear, "are you folks having a good day?"

"Ooh yes," the children chorused, "we had hot potatoes!"

He put an arm round his wife and round me and gave us both a smacking kiss.

"Oh yes, Charley Voice, I can see you are also having a good time. Was the beer good?" Pointedly avoiding his wife's barbed comment he proceeded to point out that his employers' carriage was across the road.

"My employers are having dinner with the Queen, among several hundred other lucky people," he told us, "and I've got to go and fetch them now and bring them back here for the next part of today's high jinks. Just you look out for me when you see the Queen's carriage because I won't be far behind with my party. So cheerio then, I'll see you later." And with a wave he was off.

I could see that Harry was beginning to get a bit bored with all the hanging about but when he managed to put his foot into some horse dung a few minutes later it took his mind off the tedium although his Mam was not best pleased. "Oh Harry what am I going to do with you. Whatever will you get up to next? What have I done to deserve a son like you?"

Trying to calm her down I said, "There's such a lot of it lying around today as more horses than usual are in the streets. I expect the road sweepers are trying to get it cleared up as quickly as they can."

Soon there were more exciting things to keep our minds occupied as half a dozen trumpeters arrived and took up their position on the steps at the side of the dais. Then some important people strutted into view and three little girls arrived clutching posies of hothouse flowers that they would present to the Queen, Princess Beatrice and the Mayor's wife.

Now a wave of cheering could be heard and we knew that the Queen was on her way up Corporation Street. The trumpeters played a magnificent fanfare as the Queen's carriage stopped not far away from us. With much bowing and curtseying from the dignitaries Her Majesty was escorted to the dais and the three little girls presented their posies.

"She's not going to lift that heavy stone is she?" Harry asked incredulously.

"Don't be silly, stupid. She's just going to tap it or something." Alice said in a superior way to her little brother.

"Now, now, you two," I said, "Can you see your Pa over there?"

"Cor," Harry said, "He's in the Queen's procession. Is he important?"

"All fathers are important," I replied, and then thought about mine and felt that there must surely be exceptions.

Eventually the speeches and ceremonies were over and it was time to make our way back but for a change this time we made our way to one of the cable trams that had been running between Handsworth and town for the last two years. In the crowds I had seen a familiar face and recognised my brother William with his wife, Amelia who was expecting again. They had been married for eight years and had three children already.

"Hello Amelia, hello William," I said. "I haven't seen you for quite a while."

"No, but we've been hearing about you from our Ma. You lost your job, didn't you?"

"Well, yes but we won't talk about that now."

"And Ma told us you were courting. So what's his name then?"

"Oh my, word does get around doesn't it? Well it's Evan and I'm here today with his mother, sister and brother. So let me introduce you to his mother. Here is Mrs Voice."

"Hello," Evan's Mam said, "Have you been enjoying your day?"

"Yes," Amelia said but my feet are killing me. I'll be glad to have a sit down."

"Where have you left the children?" I asked.

"Our Ma is looking after them," William replied, "so we're just off to pick them up now. It's handy leaving them with her as we live so close. Anyway we'd best be off. Ta'ra Susannah. Good afternoon Mrs Voice."

"Another one is due soon," I said turning to Evan's mother, "and then she'll have had four babies in eight years."

"Well that's about normal my dear. Most women have a baby every other year, sometimes every year. Some of them die and though it's sad in a way it makes one less mouth to feed."

I remembered what my mother had told me about her mother having so many children and then finally dying in childbirth. It filled me with horror. With that and the story of how my father had practically raped her on their wedding night, I wasn't at all sure that I wanted to get married even to Evan who I was starting to grow very fond of. But when I looked at his parents and how much they loved each other I wondered if maybe there was another way. Looking back that was a very good day. I always enjoy being with Evan's mother. She is such a dear lady.

Florence and I were still going to Carr's Lane Church quite regularly and she mentioned to a few of her lady friends that I was looking for work as a housemaid.

As it was one of the leading non-conformist churches in the town I, from my lowly position in society, always felt it was a place that mainly the great and the good went to, particularly the great. Did these non-conformist leaders of Birmingham society actually go to church to be seen as the upright citizens that they undoubtedly were or did they really go for spiritual guidance? My cynicism was influenced by my own feeling of insecurity and injustice at that time. I would later find out that many of these people actually did do a great deal of good.

I thought some people looked a bit askance when they heard about my search for work as a housemaid although to their credit no one asked about why I was changing my employment. It seemed to me though that when I was a teacher I was of sufficient social standing to mix with the sort of people who went to Carr's Lane but as a potential servant I was an inferior being. Well maybe that was all in my imagination. After all the great Dr Dale was interested in social reform and surely, in line with that, his thinking would be that all men were equal. Nevertheless I thought that maybe even for him, proclaiming equality for women might be going a bit far. Despite all my scepticism there were many good people there and it was through one of these, that I eventually found the sort of work I was looking for.

On Easter Sunday Evan arrived in the morning in time to escort us to church. We had decided to go to Holy Trinity at Birchfields. This was a relatively new church having been built only twenty years earlier but nevertheless it was built in the traditional Anglican style and had a pretty spire. Afterwards Florence had invited us to go back to have our Sunday dinner with her. A large piece of beef had been put in the oven before we left for church and I had been up early peeling potatoes and making the batter for the Yorkshire pudding.

After the meal I left Evan and Florence chatting in the parlour while I went to help the housemaid wash the dishes. She would have the rest of the day off and I thought she must have a beau hovering somewhere, as she was a pretty girl.

When I went back into the parlour they had decided that Evan and I should go for a walk so I fetched my coat, hat and gloves and arm in arm we went off in the direction of the new park next to St Mary's Church. It was due to be opened the following year and would be named Victoria Park after the Queen.

"What a lovely afternoon this is for a walk Evan. Now tell me what you know about this new park. Do we really need a park as we are surrounded here by fields and trees?"

"That point of view is indeed held by some people, Susannah, notably the rector of St Mary's Church here in Handsworth. Some people see him as the voice of disappearing rural Staffordshire. There was a great outcry at a public meeting held at the Council Offices in Soho Road only a few weeks ago in January when he spoke out against it saying that it wasn't needed in this rural parish. He said it would only attract the 'roughs' from Birmingham."

"Oh that's a bit hard isn't it? Even in the countryside it's good to have an area to stroll around in."

"That is true but the main concern of some of the leading people is that Birmingham is expanding so fast that eventually there won't be any countryside left round here because all the fields will be built over. So they see the grounds of Grove House as the ideal place for this new park. I think you can see from here that the landscaping has already started with the formation of broad tree-lined avenues."

"Yes I can see that this going to be a lovely place."

"The Local Sanitary Board are also in favour of the park. Having been very aware of the need for clean water supplies and efficient sewers to be established as the new suburban estates have been built in Handsworth now they see this park as a place for maintaining a green open space despite the encroaching suburbia."

"What a great improvement that will be. So it's to be healthy bodies and healthy minds then! From having taught in those poorer areas I am only too aware of the unsanitary conditions in places like Hockley and Lozells. There is so much disease there where houses are built so close together as back to backs and with a court where just a few water closets are shared between goodness knows how many houses. As you know there are terrible outbreaks of cholera and typhus. Now that its realised that clean water supplies and good sanitation can help to avoid such outbreaks it's good to know that all these areas of new housing are built to improved standards right from the start."

"I remember when we moved in from the village Castle Bromwich about twenty years ago Mam was delighted to find there was a water closet in the back porch so there was no more traipsing down the garden to the privy."

"It was the same when we lived at Inkberrow where I was born and then also when we lived in the village of Clent in Worcestershire which is where my younger brother John Thomas was born."

"Talking of younger brothers look who is coming down the road to meet us. We're not the only ones enjoying a stroll on this warm afternoon. Thomas and Annie seem to have had Harry thrust upon them to disturb their courting. Who would willingly choose a six year old to accompany them as they attempt to murmur sweet nothings to each other?"

"Well Evan, how about us doing the charitable thing and relieving them of the bumptious boy as we've already had a nice time on our own?"

"Yes I suppose you have a point there. We'll take him off with us and then we can all meet up again later for tea."

"Good afternoon Annie," Evan said raising his hat, "Are you enjoying your walk?"

"Thank you Evan, yes, up to a point." She said, smiling down at Harry.

"Hello Susannah, shall I come and annoy you now?" piped up Harry.

"Why do you think you might annoy me Harry?"

"Thomas says I'm a brat."

"Surely not?"

So bidding each other farewell Harry scampered around us as we continued down the road and towards St Mary's Church.

"Oh look what's coming down here," Harry suddenly roared, "a crowd of people riding those funny bicycles that looks like a penny and a farthing."

"Yes," Evan said, "Mind you don't get in their way. They are very difficult to control and quite dangerous. Thank goodness there is something much safer around now."

"What's that Evan?" The ever inquisitive Harry asked.

"Safety Bicycles, Harry. Look there's one over there leaning up against that wall," he said pointing across the road. Thus satisfied, if only temporarily, Harry found a stone to kick along the pavement.

"Susannah you can see why there is concern that soon no countryside will be left round here when you consider that this church was once completely in the country." Evan said as we were approaching the church. "In order to cope with the increased numbers of people moving into this area and attending church it was enlarged for the second time only about eighteen years ago."

Harry had been very good but it was time to give him some attention and I noticed something strange about his coat pocket.

"Harry, what's that bulge in your pocket? Get it out, let's have a look at it."

"Here you are Susannah." He said putting his hand in his pocket and drawing the object out.

"It's a spinning top. Do you know how to play with it?"

"It's too difficult."

"Give it to me. Let's see if we can make it work."

After that we had some fun with the spinning top and kept Harry amused until it was time to go back to Wellington Road for tea and the usual Sunday evening sing song round the piano.

One day in late April Florence received a short note in the post from a lady of her acquaintance who said that she was looking for a new live-in maid and did Florence think that I would be suitable for this position.

"Look Susannah, I've had this letter from Mrs Robertson. You've seen Mr and Mrs Robertson and their family at Carrs Lane Church haven't you? For many years her husband has owned a factory that makes bedsteads. Mr James Robertson campaigns for social reform and is also a town councillor. George Cadbury is another social reformer and before he moved his cocoa and chocolate production out to Bourneville from his factory in Bridge Street he reduced working hours. But I'm not sure that James Robertson went quite as far as George Cadbury did twenty years ago when he had his workers starting at six in the morning so that they would go to their beds early and thus avoid the temptations prevalent in the town in the evening hours. As George Cadbury is a Quaker I think the avoidance of the evils of alcohol was uppermost in his mind. Anyway back to Mrs Robertson who wants to know if I would recommend you as a maid. Would you like me to write back to her and give you a glowing report?"

I felt sad in some ways about this, partly because it would mean leaving Florence's house where I had been so well treated and where she had become my friend, but also because it would confirm my more lowly position in society. But looked at more pragmatically I realised that this had to be the next step forward so I put on a brave face and said,

"Yes I would like that but if I am successful in getting the position it will mean leaving you and that will be sad as you have been so good to me."

"It has been my pleasure my dear. Well that's decided so I will write back to her immediately."

Within a few days Mrs Robertson had replied and requested that I would go to see her at her house on Church Road in Edgbaston. At the appointed time I caught the train from Perry Barr into Birmingham and then at New Street Station travelled on another train out to Edgbaston where the station was very conveniently placed not far from Mrs Robertson's beautiful home. I felt very apprehensive as I walked up the tree-lined drive. I had never seen, let alone entered a house of such grand proportions as this. I wondered nervously if anyone was watching my progress up the drive from one of the many windows. It certainly seemed possible because when I reached up to pick up the brass knocker on the front door it was opened by a manservant. He asked my name and, when I gave it, knew immediately why I was there and said that I was to wait in the morning room and Madam would be down in a few moments.

He ushered me across the spacious oak floored hall where I noticed a very beautiful arrangement of spring flowers on a polished oak table. Something told me that before long I might be the person polishing that table.

The morning room was at the back of the house overlooking extensive lawns and neat beds planted with shrubs and perennials and a beautiful display of yellow and red tulips. Trees were spaced here and there and the fresh green of the leaves showed that spring was now far advanced. I thought what a charming place this was and began to feel that if its owner found me acceptable I would be very lucky to work here.

After waiting for a few minutes I heard footsteps approaching and as Mrs Robertson swept into the room with her skirts rustling on the polished floor I turned to face her. When she indicated that I should take a seat I thought her rather imperious look belied the gentleness of her manner.

"Good morning Miss Hall. I see you have been admiring the garden. It gives me great joy and also provides flowers for the house as you may have seen when you passed through the hall."

"Yes madam, I thought they were very beautiful."

"Now I need to spend a few moments with you to see if working in this house is what you want to do. We have a housekeeper and she will tell you, as a housemaid, what your duties are. A uniform and food are provided and there is sleeping accommodation in the attic for you. The pay is £16 per year."

I realised that the pay was less than the twenty pounds a year I had been paid as a pupil teacher but since it included board, lodging and uniform it was very comparable.

"I have been told in confidence by Miss Smith that you were a trusted and reliable teacher and were summarily dismissed from your job solely because of your father's misdemeanours. She has also told me that during the four years or so you have been living with her she has observed you to have an exemplary character. I want to assure you that whatever your father has done will have no influence on whether I employ you or not. Your success here will rest entirely on your own merits."

"I am grateful for that madam, and am glad that you already know about my background. It has been a great disappointment to me not to be able to continue teaching."

"Do you think you would like to work here?"

"Yes, madam, I would like to very much and I would consider myself very fortunate to work for you."

"Good. Now I will ask the housekeeper, Mrs Mason, to come and show you around the house. You may expect a letter from me within a few days."

And so saying she pulled a bell cord situated near the fireplace and within a few moments Mrs Mason had arrived. I was introduced to her and after saying goodbye to Mrs Robertson I followed Mrs Mason to the kitchen quarters next to which she had her own sitting room.

"Come and sit at the table Susannah and we'll have a cup of tea while I tell you about life in this house and what your duties will be."

The atmosphere became less formal and as we sat there drinking tea she told me about the members of the household.

"Mr and Mrs Robertson are very considerate employers but are sticklers for perfection as so they should be. Mr

Robertson has his manservant who doubles up as a butler and so deals with all the wine and glasses as well as answering the door and he looks after Mr Robertson's and the boys' clothes."

"I have met him already then?"

"Yes, he opened the door when you arrived."

"Mrs Robertson has her own maid who helps her to dress and looks after her clothes. She's the one who has all those fiddly buttons to fasten down the back of her dress and on her boots."

"Does she have to wash and mend clothes too?"

"Yes that's right but most of the clothes for the family go to the laundry although Mrs Robertson likes her maid to wash any particularly delicate articles such as those with lace on."

"If I do get offered this job shall I be the only housemaid?"

"No, we also have Rose and, like her, your day will start at six in the morning with laying the fires. Much of the rest of your long day will involve general cleaning, scrubbing floors and polishing silver. But, unlike Rose, your duties will also involve cleaning the children's rooms and looking after the girls' clothes and getting the girls ready for school."

I was glad to hear that I was going to have some contact with children.

"There are four children in this family." Mrs Mason continued, "Two boys, James is seventeen and Richard is fifteen, who attend King Edwards School in New Street and travel to school on the train. The girls, Rachel and Elizabeth, are twelve-year-old twins and attend Edgbaston High School for Girls. Usually Mrs Robertson walks the girls to the school which is not far away at the junction of Hagley Road and Harborne Road or they go in the carriage if it is wet but occasionally, due to her important social and charitable commitments, someone else in the household will have to step in so it might be you."

"I would enjoy that."

"We also have a cook, Mrs Sharp and the kitchen maid, Sally. Mr and Mrs Robertson do a lot of entertaining and there are times when it's all hands to the plough so you may find yourself waiting at table from time to time."

"Well that will be something quite new to me. I have to confess that I have never been in such a large house as this and it will all seem very strange at first."

"Don't you worry. If Mrs Robertson does offer you the job it will be because she thinks you will learn quickly to do what is expected of you."

"You may have seen the coach house in the grounds." Mrs Mason finished drinking her tea and went on, "That is the domain of Mr Brown who looks after the two horses and the family carriage which these days is not used for long distances as travel by train has become much more comfortable. So mainly it is used to take people to and from the station or around town. The stables are adjacent to it and he and his wife live in rooms above them. She helps in the house too from time to time. He also works in the garden aided by two boys who come in daily. Almost all of the vegetables for our use in the house are grown here. The glasshouse is Mr Brown's pride and joy. He grows tomatoes, grapes and peaches and sometimes is able to produce melons. Now I'm going to show you round."

And so I had a tour of the grandest house I had ever seen. There were several reception rooms, a library, and a huge dining room all furnished beautifully and with deep soft carpets and heavy, rich materials draping the windows. Upstairs there were numerous bedrooms and bathrooms with luxurious baths and hot and cold running water. There were even water closets inside the house. Not many homes had such advanced plumbing in the 1880s.

The simply furnished bedroom that might soon be mine was in the attic. It was dry and comfortable so there was nothing there I could complain of. There were two beds in there so I realised I would be sharing a room with Rose. She had arranged a few knick-knacks on the side table. There was a cupboard for our clothes and a bowl and ewer on the washstand and a chamber pot under each bed.

As I made my way back to the train and thence to Florence's house I couldn't help but contrast the living conditions of the Robertson family with the poor in such areas as Hockley and Lozells. Why did life have to be so unfair?

I knew the Robertsons were members of the group of people in Birmingham with philanthropic ideas. Yes, part of the group I had regarded as the great and the good of

Carr's Lane, I remembered; part of the group of people who really were trying to improve the living conditions of the poor people of the town.

Florence was keen to hear how my morning had gone.

"Now tell me all about it." She asked as I was taking off my coat, hat and gloves. So over our mutton chops and bread and butter pudding I recounted as much as I could remember about the house and its occupants. She was interested to hear about the schools the children went to.

"You may remember, Susannah, seeing King Edwards School in New Street. It's a very impressive Gothic styled building. And the new girls' school in Edgbaston was started ten years ago by a group of people who felt that girls' education was just as important as that for the boys."

"Good for them," I replied, "Things are moving in the right direction in some ways."

Evan called for me as usual on Sunday afternoon and as we walked towards his home in Wellington Road I told him that I was probably going to work for Mrs Robertson in Edgbaston.

"I'm afraid as a maid my time off will be very limited. I will only get half a day a week."

"I shall come over on the train and see you on your half day then."

"It doesn't look as if I shall be able to come over for your musical evenings anymore."

"Well we'll have to see how that works out. It will be a shame if you are unable to come at all."

"I'm here today so I'm determined to enjoy it." And I did.

I received the usual warm welcome from the family and we gathered round the piano after tea and sang all our favourite songs. Evan looked at me pointedly as his mother was playing 'Come into the Garden Maud' when we got to the line about the young man calling for his love at the garden gate. And later, when Evan was playing Arthur Sullivan's 'Lost Chord', his mother had to dab her eyes when we were singing about 'Death's Bright Angel'.

"You'll have to excuse me Susannah. I get a bit emotional sometimes about my old Mam who passed on four years ago. She'd gone blind and was living with my sister Jane in the hamlet of Bahaithlon near Sarn, not far from Kerry where I grew up. It's a wonderful spot and high up on the hills behind the cottage you can see for miles on a clear day, as far as the high mountains. Some say you can even see as far as Cader Idris. I do miss my hills and mountains and the clear air. Bahaithlon is near the old drovers' road from Kerry through to Myndtown over the border in Shropshire. She was born at Myndtown and behind the farm where she grew up the track leads right up onto the Long Mynd. I used to love going there as a child. That's where my heart is sometimes, up in the clear air where the larks rise up into the blue sky and the sheep graze.

Many of the songs were very melodramatic but we loved gathering round the piano and singing them. Alice had a very pretty voice and her mother often asked her to sing the Welsh song 'David of the White Rock'. She said it reminded her of her home in Wales.

We all knew Thomas was courting Annie and often she would be one of the Sunday evening singers too. So we had a bit of fun singing the Northumbrian sea shanty 'Billy Boy' and all looked at Annie while we were singing 'Is she fit to be your wife?' We knew that Annie would make Thomas a grand wife as she had been looking after her father, four brothers and her sister since her mother had died. And Annie knew that we knew, so she took it all in good part. On that particular Sunday evening we finished with the hymn 'The day Thou gavest Lord is ended'. We were reminded of the ever-expanding empire of Her Majesty Queen Victoria, our Queen Empress.

As o'er each continent and island
The dawn leads on another day,
The voice of prayer is never silent,
Nor dies the strain of prayer away.

Eventually I had to bid them all goodbye, not quite knowing when I would see them again.

"You're always welcome here Susannah. Come back as soon as you can. God bless you my dear." Evan's Mam said as she gave me a big hug. What a dear soul she is.

As usual Evan walked me home and it seemed very likely that it would be for the last time to Florence's house. He came in for a few minutes and she tactfully left us alone to say our goodbyes in the front parlour.

"Susannah, may I kiss you my dear?" Evan asked me, undeterred by Florence's father looking down on us severely from the photograph on the top of the piano. I had been hoping for some time that he would so I just smiled and nodded my head. He was so gentle even though his moustache tickled a bit. Afterwards I held up my face to be kissed again and we embraced each other and wonderful feelings of love flowed between us. I had never known anything like this before.

"Goodbye, my dear," he said after a few minutes. I heard him call out goodnight to Florence as he went into the hall. When she came into the room a few moments later she caught me shedding a few tears.

"What's this Susannah, a lovers' tiff? I hope not."

"Oh no quite the opposite. I think I've just fallen in love. I'm happy and sad at the same time and I feel uncertain because I am launching out into the next stage of my life."

"Just try to keep calm my dear. I'm sure it will all work out all right."

****

Part Three

A Different World

Within a few days I had a letter from Mrs Robertson saying that she would like to offer me the job. So a short time later I left Florence's home and moved to the Robertson's lovely home in Edgbaston. I was sorry to leave her but we remained friends for many more years.

The new life I had been so uncertain about started one Sunday evening when I carried my bag up to the small attic bedroom I was to share with Rose for the next three years. She seemed a pleasant girl but was very shy. However she was friendly and we went downstairs to have supper together in the room next to the kitchen. After supper Mrs Robertson sent for me and when I went to her in the morning room there were two lively looking girls at her side. "Susannah I'm glad you have joined this household and I hope you will be happy here. As you know part of your work will involve helping to care for my daughters so I want you to meet them now."

"Good evening Susannah," they said in unison and I wondered if, as twins, they did everything together.

"Good evening Miss Rachel and Miss Elizabeth. I'm looking forward to my work with you."

"That starts tomorrow after breakfast Susannah when you will go to their bedroom and help them get ready for school. So I want the girls to take you to their room now and show you where their things are."

"Yes madam," I said, and so with the girls leading the way we went across the hall and up the main staircase to their room.

Rachel opened the door, "Here's our room Susannah, there's our wardrobe and we each have a chest of drawers by our beds."

"And here is our book case and it has a shelf for our painting things too." Elizabeth joined in.

"What are your favourite books?" I asked.

"Oh I'm reading Black Beauty at the moment," Elizabeth said.

"And I'm reading Little Women," added Rachel.

"I remember enjoying those stories too. I'll be up here in the morning to help you get ready for school." I said, "Goodnight."

"Goodnight Susannah!" they chorused as one.

As it began to get dark Rose and I carried a candle upstairs and went to bed. It would be an early start next morning. We said goodnight to each other, blew out the candle and settled down. I lay awake for a while before I could get to sleep. It was all so strange and different but I knew I would just have to get used to the change in my circumstances. As always before I went to sleep my thoughts turned to Evan and I said a prayer asking God to keep him safe from harm.

At six o'clock the following morning Rose and I put on our housemaids uniforms. There was a black dress with a long full skirt and a white starched apron to cover it. The dress had a detachable plain white collar and cuffs. There would be lace ones for special occasions. It was finished off with a plain white frilly cap that would be exchanged for a lace one should the need arise. If I needed to leave the house on any errands I had a dark grey coat to wear with a plain bonnet. Always of course outside I would wear gloves. I descended the back stairs and presented myself to Mrs Mason and awaited instructions.

"Now first of all you'll have to put on a dark sacking apron and lay all the fires. You know how to sweep out the ashes first don't you? And then put paper and kindling ready for the fires to be lit. Coal will need to be fetched and put in the scuttle at the side of the fireplace. You'll need a bucket of water and a cloth to wash the hearth with. Rose will show you where to find everything, won't you Rose?"

"Yes Mrs Mason."

"The fire in the dining room will need to be lit straight away so that it's warm in there when the family come down for breakfast. Although it's early summer it can still be chilly and they like a warm room to have breakfast in. You'll need to dust in there as well but you can do that and watch the fire at the same time."

"Yes Mrs Mason, I'll begin that now."

Rose and I moved quietly round the house so that we

would not disturb the family. I had been told that whenever we encountered them we were to make ourselves as invisible as possible by standing to one side or moving away altogether. While I was busy with the fires Rose was cleaning the morning room so that it would be ready for Mrs Robertson when she wanted to use it after breakfast. Although I had heard that a useful tool called a carpet sweeper had been invented about ten years earlier there wasn't one in this household yet, so damp tea leaves were sprinkled on the carpet, which were then swept up with a dustpan and brush.

When I had laid all the fires and washed the hearths I removed the dark sacking apron and finished cleaning the dining room. Rose had already cleaned the morning room and started on the drawing room so I went in to help her finish it. In the drawing room a feather duster had to be used for picture frames and articles of furniture that were too high for us to reach. The rest of the furniture had to be polished with beeswax polish scented with lavender. Ornaments had to be carefully lifted up and dusted. This was something I was nervous about doing as there were many pieces of beautiful Wedgwood china in the house and I dreaded dropping any of them.

By the time we had finished the first part of our work we were ready for our breakfast. The hot tea and bread and dripping were very welcome. But there was no time for sitting long over it as Mrs Mason came in and said,

"The children have finished their breakfast; Susannah I want you to go upstairs and help them get ready for school. They need to leave in twenty minutes."

Making sure I looked respectable I ran up the back stairs, went along the landing and knocked on the girls' bedroom door.

"Good morning Miss Rachel and Miss Elizabeth. I've come to see that you have everything you need before you set out for school."

"Good morning Susannah." Rachel said, "It's interesting meeting a new maid. I hope we are going to like you. The last one was mean and interfered with our things."

"Well," I said with a smile," I don't think I shall interfere too much but I do have to clean your room so if you try to put your things away then I won't be able to interfere with them."

"Rachel's a bit bossy Susannah. Don't be frightened of her." Said Elizabeth.

"Is there anything in particular you want me to help you with before you go to school?" I said as I smiled back at her.

"We're supposed to have our hair in plaits. Would you do that for us? Sometimes we do each other's but we argue and then it goes wrong," Rachel added.

"Yes I can do that but we must hurry because your mother will be coming for you quite soon. Who is going to be first?"

"I am," said Rachel and she came and stood in front of me with a hairbrush and a ribbon. Her hair was relatively tangle free so the brush went easily through it and she stood patiently while I divided her dark wavy hair into three parts, plaited it and tied it off neatly at the end with the dark blue ribbon she had given me.

"Thank you," she said politely.

Then it was Elizabeth's turn.

"Oh dear Miss Elizabeth. What have you been doing to this? It's full of tangles. It's going to pull a bit while I try to sort it out." She was very good and only said, 'Ouch!' a couple of times. Her hair was curlier than Rachel's but eventually it was sorted out and she had a nice thick plait, which would keep her hair tidy for the day. Mrs Robertson came in just as the girls had finished putting on their coats and hats.

"The girls look smart this morning, Susannah. I like their plaits."

"Thank you madam."

When they had gone I had to clean their room and then the two rooms that the boys occupied. I picked up clothes, putting some ready for the laundry and some away in drawers and cupboards. Then the carpets had to be cleaned and the furniture polished.

All the children had books in their rooms. The girls had Anna Sewell's Black Beauty and Little Women as I had already been told but there were also Alice in Wonderland by Lewis Carroll, The Water Babies and folk tales like Grimms Fairy Tales. The boys had books about explorers, adventurers and pirates. I found out later that Robert

Louis Stevenson's Treasure Island and Coral Island by R.M Ballantyne were favourites of theirs. They wouldn't realise for some time that I, unlike many housemaids, was quite widely read.

While I was cleaning the children's rooms and bathroom Rose was cleaning Mrs Robertson's room and Mr Robertson's dressing room and bathroom. Then the stairs had to be brushed and banisters dusted. The oak floor of the hall and the beautiful oak table where a vase of flowers always stood had to be polished. The kitchen and scullery floor had to be scrubbed. Rose was a hard worker and Mrs Mason seemed pleased with our morning's efforts.

As I sat down to eat my dinner I was comparing my morning's work with the work I had done as a teacher. I concluded that this was just hard physical drudgery but teaching involved a large emotional input. Furniture and floors were inanimate objects but children were living beings with hopes, fears, pain and happiness, all of which a teacher had to interact with as well as teaching them how to read, write and do arithmetic.

The homes of the children I had taught were in stark contrast to this home. Rachel and Elizabeth and the two boys had no idea about the lives of poor children living only a few miles away from their own comfortable home. As they went off to school in the morning well dressed, well shod and having had a good breakfast there were children not far away going out onto the streets with rags on their backs and no shoes on their feet and no breakfast inside them. But Mrs Robertson knew about the sufferings of the poor as in her charitable work she was much concerned with the welfare of those poor families.

When her children had read the Water Babies they would have thought that poor Tom was just a character in a story. They would not have realised that Charles Kingsley had written that book to expose the malpractice of small boys being sent up chimneys. Just as Charles Dickens through his many books and articles had campaigned for children's rights, education and other social reforms. And indeed here at Birmingham Town Hall where he gave the first public reading of 'A Christmas Carol' on 27th December 1853 he had followed it up three days later with a second reading when the seat prices were reduced so that the working people of Birmingham would have a chance to attend.

In the afternoon as Rose and I were cleaning some of the silver she overcame her shyness and started to tell me about herself.

"How long have you been here Rose?" I asked her gently.

"I'm sixteen now so I've been here two years."

Four years younger than I am I thought.

"Have you got any brothers and sisters?"

"I did have a brother but I don't know where he is now." She replied with such a sad look on her face. "When we was little me mum had to put us in the workhouse because she had no money. Me dad spent all the money, when he was in work, on drink. We was together at first but then we was split up because girls had to go in one place and boys in another. I hardly ever saw my Sam; maybe sometimes when I peeped through the gate to where the boys was I had a glimpse of him and then the time came when I never saw him at all." A tear rolled down her cheek.

"And what about your parents?"

"Oh yes they're about somewhere. Ma came to see us at first in the workhouse but then after a time she stopped coming. Sometimes I go over there when it's my half-day but it doesn't seem like she's me ma after all these years so I don't go often. Me pa's drunk most of the time."

I was beginning to realise that as Rose was telling me about her life I might need to think up a story about mine as I certainly didn't want anyone knowing about my father or about the mayhem he had caused in my life recently. I decided that if she ever asked I would say I had come from another position, which of course in a way I had.

By the time we'd finished cleaning the silver it was time to lay up the trays for afternoon tea, which would be served in the drawing room. Mr Robertson's manservant, Mr Lloyd, would carry the trays in while Rose would hover in the background and fetch extra hot water or anything else that was needed.

When the girls came home from school I went upstairs ready to collect any dirty washing, pick up shoes that needed cleaning ready for the next day and help with anything that was needed.

Black boots were exchanged for soft house shoes. Off

came the hated black school dresses and on went long sleeved white blouses and skirts that came to just below the knee. Hands needed washing to get rid of ink stains, plaits were let out again and hair needed brushing.

"Will we do Susannah?" Rachel wanted to know.

"I'm starving." Elizabeth cried, "Come on Rachel, do hurry or all the best cakes will have gone." And off they went like a whirlwind.

I was left behind to make order out of chaos. There were clothes to pick up and put away and dirty washing to take downstairs with the boots. Finally their nightgowns had to be laid on the beds and the curtains closed for the night. It seemed that Mr Lloyd would be dealing with the boys' clothes when they came in a little later. The main work of the day was now complete but we were on duty in fact until the household went to bed. Quite often we would be called upon to help wait at table especially when the family entertained.

I started working for the Robertson family in the early summer of 1887 and as the year progressed I began to settle into the work I had to do there. The warmer weather came and with it a profusion of flowers in the garden. Mrs Robertson was a very skilful flower arranger and her beautiful displays graced the reception rooms and made a welcoming sight for people entering the hall.

There were several tennis parties during the summer and the grass court was in frequent use. The family and their friends enjoyed sitting in the peaceful garden and drinking the cool lemonade that we carried out to them. And then, in August, they went away to the seaside for a month and this gave us the opportunity to give the house a thorough clean. It also gave us a little more time off.

Occasionally I visited my mother but tried to keep out of my father's way. The news of my dismissal from my teaching post and the reason for it must have been passed on to him so he was probably trying to keep out of my way too. But foremost during my afternoons off were the times I spent with Evan. Sometimes I managed to get over to Wellington Road to enjoy the musical evenings they had on Sundays and at other times Evan would come over to Edgbaston where one of our favourite places to visit was the Botanical Gardens that were nearby.

They had been established over fifty years earlier soon after Birmingham Botanical and Horticultural Society was founded. Many local politicians and leaders of industry in the Midlands and elsewhere were members of the Society and prominent among them were the Chamberlain and Nettlefold families. Joseph Chamberlain had been President of the Society just over ten years prior to the time when we were visiting the gardens. We discovered that he gave generously to the gardens and was a keen collector of orchids. He had donated many rare plants to the collection. He truly was a remarkable man.

Sometimes we were there on Sunday afternoons and were able to enjoy the concerts given from the Bandstand. These times were precious to us and our friendship blossomed into a great love and respect for each other.

The glasshouses with their interesting collections of all sorts of tropical plants, palms and tree ferns gave us welcome shelter from showers on cooler days but otherwise we were happy to stroll arm in arm around the lawns and shrubberies. In sheltered places away from prying eyes Evan would enfold me in his arms and tenderly kiss me and tell me he loved me. Never, before I met Evan, had I known the feeling of being protected and cared for that he gave me.

On warm days we spent many an hour sitting on one of the various benches in the gardens often talking about our families. Evan was interested in history and had already told me that he and his family used to live in the sleepy Warwickshire village of Castle Bromwich.

"Several generations of the family had lived there," he told me. "There was some talk in the family that Alexander and his parents had travelled down the Chester Road, a very busy coaching route, from North Wales back in the 1700s. His brother Hugh lived in the nearby parish of Coleshill where at one time he was churchwarden."

"So what did Alexander do?"

"Well he married Elizabeth Doleman and they lived in the part of the village known as Seven Acre Green. Their old cottage was one of many belonging to Lord Bradford who lived at Castle Bromwich Hall and was the main landowner there. He paid for new thatch for their cottage when it was required and also had a new well dug. They were known as Alick and Betty and seem to have been kindly treated by Lord Bradford from whom they sometimes received flour, coal, breeches and charitable donations.

"Do you think they were rather poor then?"

"Yes I think they must have been. He was only an agricultural labourer and they didn't get paid much and maybe when the weather was poor there were times when they couldn't earn anything. It was a hard life. But he had reached the good old age of eighty three when he died in 1808 and Betty was seventy-seven when she died three years earlier so it can't have been too bad."

"So who was next in the family line?"

"It was their son Thomas who also spent his life in Castle Bromwich as an agricultural labourer, firstly marrying Mary Dingly, from which marriage there was only one son who survived infancy. Probably he went to sea. Later he married Elizabeth Mander. Their son John was my grandfather."

"So a long line of Voices had lived in that village then," I said.

"Yes and by 1840, not long after my father was born the old thatched cottages, one of which Alick and Betty had lived in, had been demolished and a row of brick ones with tile roofs replaced them."

"How far away is this village?" I asked him.

"Oh not so far, about six miles and the train goes there now. Why, do you fancy going out to see where I was born?"

"Well we could, couldn't we?"

And so it happened that one sunny day we caught the train out to Castle Bromwich and wandered round the village and saw the cottage that Evan had lived in as a boy. He showed me the village school that he had attended and the Coach and Horses Pub and the cottage next door to it where his grandparents used to live and where his uncle John was still living with his wife, another Susannah. So we called in and said hello to them.

"So this is your young lady then? Said Uncle John with a twinkle in his eyes. His wife made us a cup of tea and brought out some fruit cake she had made the day before.

"It's better after a day or so isn't it? She said to me.

"It's delicious," I agreed.

As we walked back to the station I said to Evan, "That was a lovely day out. It was interesting to see where you were living when you were a boy."

"I enjoyed it too," he said, "it brought back some memories for me."

Late summer became autumn and the gardens at the Robertson's home yielded a tremendous bounty of fruit and vegetables. There were jams to be made, fruit to be bottled and pickles to be stored ready for the winter.

I heard that the wife of my brother William had given birth to another son, Albert Edward. No doubt my mother would be seeing a lot of the new baby as they lived quite close to each other in the Jewellery Quarter. Another one of my brothers, whose name was Nimrod, had entered the Royal Navy as a boy and was still away at sea. His name was very unusual but it was a long tradition in the Hall family, with their roots in Northamptonshire, to have a son named Nimrod.

And so as the evenings drew in thoughts turned to the preparations needed for Christmas. Puddings and mincemeat were made and stored in stone jars and basins and the delicious smell of spice was in the air. As the year became colder an inevitable part of my job was to bring in yet more coal for even larger fires in the house. On Christmas Eve a huge Christmas tree was erected in the hallway. The children decorated it with carved wooden figures, silver bells and little presents wrapped in coloured paper. Small candles placed on the ends of the branches would be lit on Christmas Day. The servants were called into the hall and Rachel and Elizabeth fetched presents from under the tree to give to them.

"Happy Christmas! Happy Christmas!" Everyone said to each other. Rose and I took our presents up to our attic room and carefully undid the ribbon surrounding the packages. We had both been given warm gloves and a shawl which were very welcome as we were now entering the depths of winter.

On Christmas Day itself we were up early as usual lighting fires and making the house warm and comfortable for the family. Then Rose and I were allowed to go to an early service at a local church. It was a cold, frosty morning and we put on our hats and new gloves, pulled our coats tightly about us and wrapped our warm shawls around our shoulders. The sun was rising as we walked along the streets and when its rays caught the frost on the trees we found ourselves in a sparkling fairy-tale world. We laughed at the clouds our breath made in the frosty air but the cold penetrated our boots setting our chilblains tingling. We joined in the traditional carols with gusto especially the last verse of 'O come all ye faithful',

Yea, Lord, we greet thee,
Born this happy morning,
Jesu, to thee be glory given.

And then it was out into the freezing morning again and back to the house to complete the preparations that would make this a memorable Christmas.

None of us could see into the future, thank goodness, but sadly for the Robertson family, Christmas would never be quite the same again.

1887 drew to a close and for me it had been a tumultuous year. My teaching career had abruptly finished and that was very regrettable but my current employment had turned out to be good. Also very good was my deepening relationship with Evan. We were undoubtedly in love.

Sometimes the Robertson's entertained friends and family in the evening. And in the early summer of 1888 there was great excitement in the house because the great Joseph Chamberlain was to be entertained to a sumptuous evening meal. Other Birmingham luminaries would also be present. It would be a very grand occasion indeed. This was certainly an occasion for clean uniforms with lace collars, cuffs and caps. Mrs Mason stood ready at the kitchen door to inspect us.

"Now Susannah, let's have a look at you to make sure everything is as it should be. Yes, that's good and now you

Rose. Yes, two smart young housemaids. Well done girls. Now be very careful not to spill anything and take care to anticipate whatever any of the guests may be needing."

The guests had arrived and were assembled in the drawing room. A butler had been hired for the evening and was busy carrying round a tray on which the crystal champagne glasses reflected the many lights in the chandeliers. Afterwards he confided to us that he had noticed that several of the guests being Quakers did not partake of alcoholic drinks. Rose and I thought that although Mr Lloyd might have given the impression that his nose had been put out of joint with an extra butler being hired, secretly he was very glad to have the extra help that the hired butler provided

At eight o'clock the meal was announced and Mrs Robertson, resplendent in satin and pearls, led her guests into the dining room, which was decorated with her beautiful flower arrangements. The table looked magnificent with polished silver cutlery and sparkling glasses. Mr Chamberlain, being the most important male guest, was seated on his hostess's right and the other guests were shown to their places. I didn't know who they all were but gathered that some local councillors were there and people who were known for their philanthropic works in the town. The meal was well received and the guests talked to the person on one side of them for a while and then politely engaged the person on their other side in conversation. So the evening was judged to be a great success.

I could hear snippets of conversation as I moved round

the table with the serving dishes and it seemed that one of the topics of conversation was the expansion of the British Empire of which Mr Chamberlain was wholeheartedly in favour. In the previous year when he had visited Toronto he had said, 'I should think our patriotism was warped and stunted if it did not embrace the Greater Britain beyond the seas.'

A piece of news everyone seemed delighted with was his forthcoming trip to the United States in November when his marriage to Mary Endicott would take place in Washington.

"She will be impressed by Highbury," someone said.

I'd heard of this house at Moseley he had built ten years previously. It sounded very grand indeed.

After the guests had left Mrs Robertson came to the kitchen and thanked everyone for their hard work. It had been a long hard day and we had spent many hours on our feet. Rose and I climbed wearily into our beds and fell asleep as soon as our heads touched our pillows.

The summer proceeded much as the previous one had done and in August the family went again to the seaside for a month. When they came home preparations were made for James to go to University. His father had been at one of the Oxford Colleges and it had been arranged that James would follow in his father's footsteps.

James started his university life in October and he was much missed but it wasn't until a dull November day that everyone's life was turned completely upside down.

Elizabeth awoke one morning with a sore throat and high fever. Rachel fetched her mother into the bedroom and when Mrs Robertson saw how a rash was spreading over Elizabeth's body she became very alarmed. I was called upstairs urgently and told to go to the coach house and send Mr Brown for the doctor immediately. When I had done that I went back upstairs. The girls now had separate bedrooms and Rachel was told to get dressed quickly, but not in her school clothes, and go downstairs for her breakfast.

Mrs Robertson came out of Elizabeth's room briefly and she drew me to one side where the girl would not hear what was being said. "Susannah, I have seen this rash and high fever before in some of the poorer homes I visit. I think it is the dreaded scarlet fever. We must get Rachel and Richard away from here immediately. It's very contagious." I too had seen this disease before, as it was widespread.

"My sister lives in Worcester where her husband is Dean of the Cathedral and she will have the children. I want you to pack up some clothes for Rachel and tell Mr Lloyd he is to do the same for Richard. A telegram has been sent to my sister and I want you to take them to Worcester escorted by Mr Lloyd. The children are not to come upstairs again. Now hurry and get them away from here."

Poor woman; she was distraught and with good reason as many deaths were caused by scarlet fever. In 1883-4 the Borough Hospital for Smallpox and Scarlet Fever had opened in Winson Green on the other side of Birmingham but I knew she would not want Elizabeth to go there. She would want to nurse her at home. Fortunately by now deaths from fevers were declining in Birmingham but had been as high as 1,700 a year caused by smallpox, scarlet fever, diphtheria, whooping cough and diarrhoea to mention a few.

The house we were going to was on College Green at Worcester and within an hour Mr Lloyd, the children and I, had left the Robertson home and were waiting to board the train for Worcester at New Street Station. Although Rachel and Richard did not realise the seriousness of the situation they were surprised to be suddenly leaving their home but they were also quite pleased to be going to stay with their Aunt in Worcester. They knew her well and had stayed at the house before.

"Susannah, it's in a lovely position above the River Severn and when you go across the Green before you go into the Cathedral you pass through the cloisters of the old Benedictine Monastery that once was there. You can also go down to the river through the old Watergate where there's a ferry that will take you across the river to the meadows on the other side, or from the same side you can walk along the river bank and the swans, past the old warehouses by the river and on to the lovely old bridge." Rachel happily chattered away about what they would see and do and she had no idea of the serious condition of her sister. But my thoughts were back in Birmingham with Elizabeth.

When the train arrived at Shrub Hill Station we found that the Dean had kindly sent his carriage for us and the coachman was waiting for us on the platform. While we were getting installed in the carriage Mr Lloyd went off to find a porter and arrange for the luggage to be taken out of the guard's van. The short ride from the station to College Green only took a few minutes. Rachel excitedly pointed out the Edgar Tower as we rattled underneath it over the cobblestones and onto the Green surrounded on two sides by the grand houses of important church dignitaries.

13. The Edgar Tower, Worcester

"Susannah you'll never believe this but Aunt says that during the Civil War the Royalists poured boiling lead through a hole in the roof of the tower down onto the heads of their enemies the Roundheads."

The children's Aunt greeted us with great concern but we were able to tell her little more than she already knew. We needed to be back in Birmingham as soon as possible so within half an hour the Dean's carriage returned us to the station and within two or three hours we were back in Birmingham and anxious to hear what the doctor had said

14. College Green, Worcester

15. The River Severn at Worcester

about Elizabeth's condition. The news was grim. Mrs Robertson described the rising fever; the rash spreading over her body and the nausea that Elizabeth was feeling.

"Susannah we just have to hope and pray that our darling will not be taken away from us."

She would not leave the child's side but following the doctor's instructions sponged her with tepid water to try to keep the fever down and gave her sips of lemon barley water. All that day and night and the following day the house was quiet as everybody crept around not wanting to disturb the invalid. Mrs Sharp, the cook, prepared tempting meals, which were barely touched. Rose and I continued with our normal daily round of laying fires, bringing in fuel and cleaning. For me there were no girls to tidy round after or greet as they came in from school. It was very strange.

Each day I crept into Elizabeth's room to do a little dusting and each time I went in my eyes turned to the poor child on the bed and the weary mother by her side. It was only Mrs Robertson's maid who could persuade her to rest in her own room for half an hour occasionally and then she would soon be back to see if there was any change. The doctor called three times a day and by the evening of the third day there was no improvement and he ordered that all of Elizabeth's beautiful curls be cut off. Another night passed and the poor girl became delirious. By the evening of the fourth day it was over.

Mrs Robertson could not be consoled for the loss of her beautiful daughter; Mr Robertson retreated into his study and the house was filled with the sound of the servants sobbing. How could this lovely, vibrant girl be taken so cruelly from us? Very easily I am afraid. Though loss of children was all too common among the poor, death also struck without warning in the better off households and even in Royal Households, as in the death of Prince Albert from typhoid when he was only forty-one years of age.

Elizabeth's funeral took place a week later at Edgbaston Old Church. James had returned from Oxford; a subdued Richard and Rachel returned from Worcester with Mrs Robertson's sister. Her husband had been prevailed upon to conduct the service. A dressmaker had been in and made deep mourning clothes for those of us who did not already have them.

The servants were allowed to attend the funeral providing they came back to the house quickly afterwards to attend to the food that was provided for family and friends after the burial. The coffin containing Elizabeth's body had rested in the dining room where the curtains were drawn, as was the custom. On the day of the funeral the bearers carried it out to the glass sided hearse adorned with shining brass, and drawn by four black horses with black plumes on their heads. Behind that a procession of carriages pulled by black horses conveyed the family to the church. Mrs Robertson was deeply veiled in black.

As Rose and I walked to the church we remembered the previous Christmas morning when we had come through the frost to the early service and had joyously sung 'O Come all ye faithful'. Today there was no joy. We did not have time to stay for the burial but later were told that Elizabeth had been buried in a quiet corner of the churchyard and that in due course a memorial would be erected in that spot. On the day of the funeral I had seen Rachel's wan and pinched face and my heart went out to the poor girl. I did not have a chance to speak to her until the next day when I went to her room as usual in the morning to see what I could do for her.

"Susannah I am completely lost without my twin sister. I didn't even say goodbye to her. I can't bear this. Why was she taken and not I? She was so lovely. Whatever am I going to do?" She sat on the bed crying pitifully.

I sat down next to her and put my arm round her. "There, there my dear. I think there is something you can do. Your mother is feeling just as bereft as you are. Be a companion to her and maybe you will both be able to help each other in your grief." And that is what Rachel did, bless her, and through the following months she and her mother became very close, in fact probably closer than they had ever been before.

So Christmas that year was very different from the previous one when everybody had been so jolly. Memories were too strong for the family in that house and they went to the South of France for several weeks, away from the gloom of an English winter and away from memories of the happy Christmas of twelve months ago.

And so the days moved on and a new year dawned. It was 1889. Because the house had been more or less closed up there was less work and so more time off. I spent some time with my family and saw William and Amelia's children. I was told that later in the year yet another one would join Albert Edward and his three siblings. My brother James and his wife Emily were expecting their third child. Nimrod was still at sea and my younger brother John was courting Clara. But my fourteen-year-old sister

Mary was still living with my parents in Warstone Lane. They all lived very close to each other in Hockley. My mother was very involved with helping her daughters-in-law with their children and with their hands full they were glad of any help she could offer.

As ever, my chief joy was spending time with Evan and his family. In the cold, frosty air of January, Evan would come over to Edgbaston and collect me whenever he could and arm in arm we would set off together to walk into town or stroll round the Botanical Gardens. Sometimes I was able to meet Annie in town and we enjoyed going round the shops together or stopping for a chat in a coffee shop. She confided in me that Thomas was getting increasingly passionate and she could foresee a time when it would no longer be possible to say 'no'. "Oh do be careful, Annie," I warned her, "you don't want to get yourself in the family way do you when you're not married?"

"Well no I don't but it's becoming very difficult to resist him"

"Oh you wicked girl," I said with a smile.

Eventually the Robertson family returned and tried to pick up the pieces of their lives. Rachel, now more serious, resumed her school days and Richard studied hard so that he would be able to follow his brother to Oxford. Mrs Robertson returned to her charitable activities and Mr Robertson carried on with his business affairs and in the evenings was often closeted in his study.

It became established that through the summer months I would walk Rachel to and from school. I was interested to hear what she was learning about and I was surprised one day when she said, "Susannah, I've been thinking about my future. I'd always assumed that I would follow in Mama's footsteps, marry, have children and run a successful household just like any other upper class girl but now I'm not so sure about that. I think I want to have a career and do something useful in the world. Losing Elizabeth has made me look around more and I've been learning from Mama that there are many poor people even here in Birmingham. Maybe I could teach or be a nurse. What do you think?"

"Yes there are many people who need help but I think your parents will be very disappointed if you don't follow what they have in mind for you."

"Yes that could be the case, as it was with Florence Nightingale but I think she made nursing a respectable profession for girls of my class didn't she?"

"Well you have another two or three years at school so the best thing is to work as hard as you can and to read a lot so that when you do leave school you will be as well informed as it is possible to be."

"You know I often wonder about you Susannah. You seem to be a lot better read and informed than the average housemaid."

"Do I?" I answered innocently.

But by the time Rachel finally decided what she wanted to do with her life I had left the Robertson household.

In September I had a letter from Annie asking me to meet her in town. It was always a pleasure to be with her so I looked forward to our meeting. But when I saw her face I knew that something was wrong and it filled me with disquiet. "Well I won't beat about the bush," she said. "What you warned me about has happened. I told you I wouldn't be able to resist him much longer and now I am pregnant. I don't know what I am going to do."

"Neither do I Annie. This will put the cat among the pigeons when the news gets out. Have you told Thomas yet?

"No I haven't told anybody. I wanted you to be the first to know. You are so sensible. I'm just relying on you to come up with a solution."

"Well just give me a few moments to think about this. You are by no means the first woman to find herself in this predicament. So I think, as always, it's Evan and Thomas's mother you need to go to. She'll come up with something."

The next time I saw Annie she looked a lot happier. "Susannah you were quite right in telling me to go to her. Guess what, she was pregnant when she married. As you said I'm not the first person to be in the family way on her wedding day."

"So there is to be a wedding then?"

"Oh yes, we must get married and I want to marry Thomas anyway, I love him, but it's my Pa who's being the awkward one. I think the trouble is he wants me to stay and run the household as I have since my ma died. He doesn't want Thomas taking me off somewhere else."

"Well there's an easy solution to that," I said. "Thomas will just have to move in with you, your Dad and your brothers."

"Yes I hadn't thought of that. You're right. I'll see if that is acceptable to them all."

I saw Evan at the weekend. He was fuming. "I suppose you've heard the news," he said. "Thomas is an idiot. He should have thought of where they were going to live before he got her in the family way. He's doing it all in the wrong order."

"I gather a solution has been found to the problem though," I said soothingly.

"Well yes, I have to admit that it has. But I can tell you if I wanted to marry a girl I'd make sure I had a home ready to take her to first, then marry her and do it all in the right order. Humph!"

We walked along the street. The leaves were falling now and swirled around our feet. It started to rain and we huddled together under Evan's umbrella. "What shall we do now?" I asked. "It's a bit dreary standing around here."

"Let's go into the Art Gallery." Evan said, "At least it's out of the rain."

So we turned round and walked back the way we had come, past the Chamberlain Memorial and crossed the road into the Art Gallery. He was able to leave his umbrella with the attendant near the door and then he took my hand and we climbed the stairs to the galleries above. We wandered round for a while looking at the paintings and the displays of stuffed animals and birds in their glass cases. "You know Susannah, what I'd really like to be doing today is sitting in front of my own cheerful fire with you on my knee."

"Yes I think that would be much better than hanging around in the rain. But you haven't got your own fire."

"No that's a problem. I think I'm beginning to feel envious of Thomas after all. They're getting married in January and although they won't actually have their own home they'll be together all the time."

"Yes, apart from having to go to work and share a house with her father and her four brothers they won't be hanging around in the rain wondering where to go will they?"

We walked past a few more stuffed birds.

"Susannah."

"Yes Evan."

"I love you my dear girl."

"I love you too Evan."

"Do you think we'd like to be together all the time like Thomas and Annie?

"I think that would be very acceptable." I said with the

corners of my mouth twitching, making a guess at what was coming next.

"Susannah."

"Yes Evan."

"I love you very much and want to spend the rest of my life with you and caring for you. Will you marry me my dearest girl?"

"Darling Evan that would make me so happy. Yes of course I will."

We found a convenient stuffed bird that would hide us from prying eyes and Evan enfolded me in his arms and gently kissed me. I was so happy now to be promised in marriage to this dear, kind man. Although the convention was that he should then have gone to see my father and ask his permission to marry his daughter I didn't feel it was necessary to ask the old rogue's permission, so instead we went to Wellington Road and announced our engagement that evening. Evan's Pa brought out some glasses and a bottle of blackberry wine from the previous year and our good health was drunk.

"Dear Susannah," his Mam said, "I shall love having you as my daughter in law." His Pa looked very pleased as well and his twinkly eyes showed us that he was happy. The day ended with Evan taking me back to the Robertson house where under the shelter of the trees at the end of the path he gave me a lovely kiss. "Having said harsh words about Thomas earlier I must now set about finding somewhere for us to live and then we can decide on a date for the wedding."

"An Easter wedding would be perfect," I said.

"But there is something we must do quite soon," Evan said, "You must have an engagement ring and as I am a jeweller I shall make it for you."

"Evan that will be very special."

So the following week when it was my half day Evan met me in town and we went to his tiny workshop in the Jewellery Quarter. I had not been there before and I found it fascinating. Evan explained to me that formerly there had been large detached villas in the streets near St Paul's Church. They had been surrounded by gardens and there had been allotments for the workers but as the area became famous for the production of jewellery in the mid-1800s, the gardens gradually became built up with workshops and the allotments were built over too. But there were also some purpose built jewellery factories such as the ones in Warstone Lane where my parents lived and where my father had his job as a night watchman. There were diamonds, precious stones and gold that needed guarding.

We went down Livery Street and turned off into a maze of streets near St Paul's church. We went into an alleyway at the side of what had been one of the large detached houses Evan had been telling me about. At the back of it the garden had been completely built over with another building with a small yard in front of it. "Come this way," he said, and we climbed some steps and went through a door at the top. He led me into a series of small rooms where men were working at the peg benches. These had a cut out where the men sat with their tools around them and mounted diamonds and precious stones to make beautiful rings. We stopped by one man and Evan introduced me to his friend George Nicholls. He stood up and said, "I'm glad to meet you Miss Hall. And glad to hear about your engagement. I understand Evan is going to make you a beautiful ring?"

"Yes that is so. Aren't I lucky?" I replied with a smile.

We continued on down the long room and there at the end was Evan's own peg bench in the room that he had told me about, and the gas light so that he could see the fine detail of the work that as a jeweller mounter he had to do. He fetched some diamonds from their safe storage place and put them on a black velvet display cushion so that I could get some idea of what the finished ring would be like.

"Susannah, if you would like it I suggest you have three diamonds in a row with the central one slightly larger than the outer two. What do you think of that?"

"I think it's going to be wonderful and I also think you are a very clever craftsman."

"So it's going to be a wonderful ring for a wonderful girl is it?"

I had no opportunity to reply to that for he caught me up in his arms and kissed me passionately.

"Hold on," I said when he eventually released me, "let's

not get carried away."

"Pity," he replied as he went to put the diamonds away, "So roll on Easter then!"

A week later I went over to his house one Sunday evening and he gave me my lovely ring. The diamonds sparkled and the gold shone. He put it on my finger and I was thrilled and proudly showed it off to his family who were duly impressed.

Another Christmas passed and the new year of 1890 was upon us. Thomas and Annie were married on 16th February. It was a happy occasion and although Annie was very obviously pregnant we were all glad to see them wed. She would make Thomas a splendid wife.

At that time luck was on our side because the house next door to Evan's parents became available for us to rent and so the date was set for Monday April 7th. So I had my wish and it was to be an Easter wedding. We decided to get married at Trinity Church, Birchfields; I moved back in with Florence for a month before the wedding. In some ways I was sad to leave the Robertson family. They had been so kind to me and I had been with them during such a traumatic time of their lives. Mrs Robertson generously presented me with a beautiful piece of white satin with which to make my wedding dress. I was delighted to have such a magnificent piece of material. On my last evening in their home Rachel came to me and gave me a big hug. "Susannah I feel you are more a friend than a servant. You have given me such encouragement about my future." Some years later I read in the paper that she had fulfilled her ambition and become a nurse for a few years and then there had been a very fashionable wedding. So I suppose she had followed her dreams in more ways than one.

Florence loved having me back in my old room in her house and I loved being there. She entered into the wedding preparations with great enthusiasm. There was plenty of sewing to be done for my trousseau and for household articles and often in the afternoons we sat by the fire doing the sewing and chatting about old times. "I was right you see, all those years ago. Romance was in the air." She said to me with a smile on her face.

I also enjoyed going over to Wellington Road and sitting with Evan's Mam while we did our sewing and she chattered on about the past. I was going to like living next door to her. Alice helped me make my wedding dress. I was delighted that she did this because by now she was a very promising dressmaker. Together we chose a style with a tiny waist, high neck, long sleeves and a short train. I would be wearing a veil held in place by a simple floral band. She and my sister Mary would be my bridesmaids and Evan's sister Lizzie would be my maid of honour and it had been arranged that she, as well as my father, would sign the register as witnesses to the marriage. They would all wear blue satin dresses to match the blue ribbon in my bouquet.

As the time for the wedding drew near I became very tense. There was so much to do. Evan's Pa arranged with his employer to borrow the carriage that would collect Florence, my attendants and me and take us to the church. After the ceremony it would take the bridal party to the photographic studio in Handsworth although finally it was decided to hire an additional carriage for that to accommodate everybody. Then after that we would all go back to Wellington Road for our wedding breakfast which Evan's Mam, Lizzie and Alice had arranged. My mother was helping with that too.

We had been to the church on the three Sundays before Easter and heard our banns read. I had long thought it must be nerve wracking for the bridal couple waiting with bated breath to see if anyone would stand up and place an objection to the marriage. I even had nightmares about this happening to me. I would wake in the middle of the night when a stern voice said, "Objection to the marriage! This is the daughter of William Hall. She is tarred with the same brush." Evan laughed when I told him about my nightmares, "Oh dear Susannah, absolutely no one is going to do that." But I was not totally reassured. It was just another worry to add to my list.

We went to church on Easter Sunday, the day before our wedding, and it looked beautiful. The parish ladies had decorated the church with spring flowers. On every windowsill there were primroses, violets, wild daffodils and fresh green leaves. I couldn't help feeling excited and I thought to myself, "This is how it will look tomorrow when I walk down the aisle for my marriage to dear Evan."

So the day dawned. Lizzie, Alice and Mary arrived early in the morning to help me dress. Florence helped where she could and my portmanteau was packed ready to be collected on our way to the station later. Florence came in to view the finished ensemble before we set out on the short journey to the church. "My dear you look beautiful," she said, "Evan is a very lucky man."

The carriage arrived with my father in it for he would be walking down the aisle with me to give me away. He looked a bit nervous and when we were on our own for a few moments he said hesitatingly in his gruff voice, "Susannah, you are a lovely daughter and a very beautiful bride. I wish you all the best for a long and happy marriage with Evan. I'm afraid I haven't been the best husband in the world to your poor mother. If I had my time again I would make a better job of it."

That was a long speech for my father to make and I could tell it came from his heart. I was moved to give him a quick kiss on the cheek. My heart was too full to say anything.

Evan's father had raided his employer's hothouse for white gardenias and Lizzie had added scented lilies of the valley and a blue ribbon, making me a beautiful bouquet. Mary picked it up and handed it to me. I held it to my face and breathed in the heavenly scent. We left Florence's house with my three attendants carefully holding up my train and veil and placing them around me in the carriage. My Pa rode up front with Evan's Pa who had turned round and beamed at me as I got in the carriage. "Susannah, you're the world's most beautiful bride. No wonder the sun is shining on you."

Off we went with the horses neatly picking up their hooves and the carriage wheels rumbling over the cobbles. Evan's Pa had threaded ribbons through the horses' manes and brushed their coats until they shone and oiled their hooves. No doubt we were a pretty sight for onlookers but

I was feeling very nervous. When the Curate met us at the church door he smiled at me and said, "I shall precede you, and when I turn at the altar steps to face the congregation it will be time for you to walk down the aisle."

As I stood there I could see the members of our families who had gathered to see us married. On the left at the front was my mother who turned when she realised we had come into the church. She gave me an encouraging smile for she knew I was nervous. In the row behind her was my brother William with Amelia his wife and their three eldest children William, James and Alice. The younger ones Albert and Ernest had been left at home with Amelia's mother. Seated behind them were my brother James and his wife Emily and their two eldest children Lillian and Herbert. Their baby Ernest was being taken care of elsewhere. My other two brothers, Nimrod and John Thomas and my father's brother James and his wife Maria, fortunately without their numerous children, completed my family group. Florence was sitting next to them.

Near the altar rail on the other side of the aisle Evan was resolutely facing the front for it was bad luck to turn and see your bride walking down the aisle. His brother Thomas at his side had turned as we came into the church and then gave Evan a reassuring nod as if to say, "It's alright Evan she's here." Their mother was in the front pew with ten year old Harry, all spruced up for the occasion and a space beside her for Evan's Pa who was securing the horses and would join her in just a moment. In the same row was Annie and I was delighted to see her there so soon after the birth of baby Charles Thomas who had arrived on the thirteenth of March.

Evan's eldest sister, Tilly, was in the pew behind her parents having come all the way from Cheshire where she was a housemaid at Combermere Abbey. In the same row was Lizzie's fiancé Henry Hurst. In from Castle Bromwich were Evan's Uncle John with his wife Susanna and his father's widowed sister Elizabeth. Behind them on both sides were all our friends and neighbours.

I nervously laid my hand on my father's arm. Lizzie, Alice and Mary were behind us. The organ was playing quietly. The Curate had turned and was facing us, the congregation stood; Evan and Thomas had moved forward to stand at the chancel steps. It was time to walk down the aisle. This was the most important day in my life, my heart started to beat faster. Within a short time Evan and I would be man and wife. I couldn't believe that the moment I had been waiting for was now upon me.

At last I was standing beside Evan. He smiled at me and as our fingers touched warmth and love flooded between us. The marriage service started.

"Dearly beloved we are gathered here in the sight of God and in the face of this congregation to join together this man and this woman in holy matrimony," the Curate's calming tones moved on through the service, "honourable estate…mystical union…. not by any to be taken lightly or wantonly….ordained for the mutual society, help and comfort… in prosperity and adversity." The words floated over me. I couldn't take it all in even though I had spent some time in the previous weeks reading through the service. Then came the moment I had been having nightmares about in case anyone stood up and said we should not be married but of course, as Evan had assured me, no-one did and all was well.

Turning to Evan the Curate said,

"Wilt thou have this woman to thy wedded wife…to love…. comfort…. honour…in sickness and in health as long as ye both shall live?" Evan said,

"I will."

Then the Curate turned to me and said,

"Wilt thou have this man to be thy wedded husband…. wilt thou obey and serve him, love, honour and keep him in sickness and in health as long as ye both shall live?"

"I will."

Then my father took my hand and gave it to Evan who made his solemn vow about loving me and looking after me until death parted us. Then it was my turn to make my solemn vow about loving him and obeying him. Thomas produced the ring and gave it to Evan, who then placed it on my ring finger with the words,

"With this ring I thee wed, with my body I thee worship, and with all my worldly goods I thee endow." We knelt down and there were prayers at the end of which the Curate pronounced us 'Man and Wife'.

Now we really were married. I looked up at my husband and longed to be taken in his arms but that would have to wait until afterwards. We went into the vestry to sign the register. I put my maiden name Susannah Hall, Evan wrote Charles Evan Voyce then Evan's sister put her signature, Sarah Elizabeth Voyce, and then my father, William Hall, added his. The Curate had filled in the details of our names and ages and that Evan was a bachelor and I was a spinster and our addresses, 219, Wellington Road for him and Birchfield Road for me. He had put our fathers' names and occupations, Charles Voyce, coachman, William Hall watchman and finally filled in his name, Edward Scott, Curate.

I took Evan's arm and our eyes met. We were both so very happy. Our first walk together as man and wife was out of the vestry and down the aisle to the church door. What a joy it was to be surrounded by our families and friends and to see their smiling faces and to know that we had their love and good wishes for our future. Outside the church there were two carriages waiting to convey us to the photographer's studio in Handsworth. When we arrived the photographer, a dapper little man with Italian origins, led us into his studio where there was a backcloth of a pleasant rural scene.

"Ze 'andsome bridegroom pleez sit 'ere," he said and Evan was shown to a chair in the centre.

"Ze beautiful bride to stand 'ere and just so," and I was put at his side and slightly to the back of him. My right hand was arranged to lie on his shoulder and the other to hold my bouquet.

"And zee other peoples to stand round the back and ze two pretty young ladies to sit on ziz stools at the front."

Lizzie stood behind Evan and to his right were his parents. On my left were my parents. Mary and Alice sat on the low stools in front of us.

The photographer told us not to smile and to keep perfectly still for the exposure time of a few seconds. He inserted a large photographic plate into his camera and disappeared under a cloth, which was draped over the camera. The shutter clicked and it was over.

"Zat ees done." he said. The photograph would be ready when we came back from our honeymoon.

After a splendid wedding breakfast at Wellington Road it was time for me to slip next door to our new home and change ready for the journey to Weston-super-Mare where we would be spending the first week of our married life together. My bridesmaids came with me and gently eased me out of my beautiful satin wedding dress. I put my bouquet in a vase of water but knew that by the time we returned it would be past its best. I put on a mid-blue travelling dress with a saucy little hat with a blue feather at the crown and a small veil draped round the brim and then there were blue kid gloves to complete the outfit.

We drove to New Street Station in style, Evan's Pa once again having been able to borrow his employer's carriage. Our families and friends had gathered outside the house to see us off. My mother became a bit weepy but big brother William put an arm round her shoulders and said, "She'll be all right Ma, don't fret." Our luggage was strapped onto the back of the carriage, people waved and called "Goodbye! Good Luck!", and we were off.

I was so happy. Here was I married to a man I adored bowling along the streets in a carriage and pair on a beautiful spring day. The colourful ribbons Evan's Pa had tied to the carriage fluttered in the breeze and bystanders waved as we passed. This was the happiest day of my life. Along we went into town through Corporation Street and down into Stephenson's Place and pulled up with a flourish in front of New Street Station. Evan handed me down and his Pa found a waiting porter to deal with our luggage. Then there was a big hug for me and he said, "Have a good time me duck. I've just got myself another lovely daughter. Look after her Evan, treat her gently."

He and Evan shook hands and then we followed the porter along to the platform for the Bristol train. New Street was a noisy, bustling station and despite it being a pleasant April afternoon it was a noisy, draughty place. The engines like huge roaring monsters dwarfed the people waiting on the platforms. Smoke billowed high into the air and swirled under the cavernous arches and steam hissed from beneath the wheels of the engines. Porters with carts piled high with luggage and mailbags shouted at people to get out of the way. The train guards called out the departure times of the trains and told people to hurry along. Everywhere it seemed streams of people were rushing for trains or leaving trains that had just arrived.

We found an empty first class compartment having treated ourselves on this special occasion. The porter who had placed our luggage in the guard's van touched his cap when he received a tip from Evan. So we climbed the narrow steps and Evan smiled at me and said, "Now my love, do you want to sit facing the engine or with your back to the engine? In other words do you want to see where we are going or where we have come from?"

"Oh Evan this is definitely the day for looking forwards I think, don't you?" So there we sat as a married couple looking forward to where we were going in every sense of the word. We didn't have to wait long; a whistle blew, doors slammed and the roaring monster started to move out of the station. Evan and I looked at each other,

"Alone at last," Evan said and looking into my eyes reached out his hand for mine. "Good afternoon, Mrs Voyce. How are you feeling?" I squeezed his hand and leant towards him,

"To tell you the truth I'm not sure how I feel. Today has gone by in such a whirl. I was so nervous to start with and I felt so strange walking up the aisle towards you with my father. Incidentally earlier I'd had quite a speech from him, an apology I suppose it was really, about him letting me and my mother down."

"Yes he had, I think, especially regarding your job."

"Well that's all water under the bridge now but it's my mother he should really have been apologising to. He's led her a merry ride all through the years. Anyway don't let's think any more about him. Yes it's been an amazing day. And here we are, married at last"

"But you haven't answered my question, have you?"

"Well I'm very happy that we are married. I'm looking forward to being with the man I love and making our home together. And how are you feeling?"

"I'm feeling I want to take you in my arms and hold you tight."

"Well I think that's a very good idea and I think you'd better get on with it in case anybody else gets into this compartment at the next station." His arms came round me and his lips found mine and for a few moments time stood still. "My darling," he whispered as he held me close, "You're mine at last."

As his arms enfolded me I felt happier and safer than I had ever been in my life before. The train had gathered speed and was now travelling out through Selly Oak and Northfield, the new suburbs to the south of Birmingham and then on into the Worcestershire countryside where orchards were frothy with apple blossom and lambs raced around together.

By the time the train reached Worcester we no longer had the compartment to ourselves and had to be content with just sitting next to each other companionably. The train stopped for a few minutes at Shrub Hill station and I sadly remembered the last time I had been there when I had taken Rachel Robertson and her brother to stay with their aunt in the Cathedral Close.

But today was not the day for remembering sadness, it was my wedding day and I was sitting by the man I loved enjoying the beautiful views from the train windows. Evan produced a map from his pocket and as we approached Tewksbury we were able to identify to the west the purple line of the Malvern Hills and to the east Bredon Hill and the slopes of the Cotswolds where they rose above the Severn flood plain. And so our journey continued to Cheltenham Spa and then to Gloucester and finally the train drew into Temple Meads Station at Bristol. "Susannah we have to wait here for half an hour until the next train leaves for Weston-super-Mare."

"Does it come into this platform?"

"No we have to change to another one so I'll just go and find a porter for our luggage and leave you here for a couple of minutes." While he was gone I gazed about me at this magnificent station, and into my mind came the well-known picture of its designer Isambard Kingdom Brunel in his stove pipe hat and I remembered that this was the first station he had designed. Evan soon returned with a porter and his trolley and we crossed to the platform from which the Weston train departed. We were looking forward to getting to our destination for it had been a long and exciting day. We were both tired by the time our train arrived at Weston-super-Mare. It was getting dark and we were glad to find that the small hotel Evan had booked for us was clean and welcoming. A light supper had been laid but I was not very hungry and could only manage a few mouthfuls. Evan looked at me anxiously, "Are you all right Susannah?"

"Yes," I said with a smile, but in truth I was feeling nervous about the wedding night. Much as I loved Evan and wanted to be a good wife to him I couldn't help feeling apprehensive. Annie had been very helpful in allaying my fears, "Just a bit of pain the first time but as you both love each other so much just as we did it's soon over." She had said comfortingly.

"I expect you are tired," Evan said, "you go up first and I'll join you in a few minutes. Don't worry about anything my love. This is a new world for both of us."

So up I went and removed my travelling clothes and hung them in the wardrobe. I donned my new lacy nightdress and stood by the window looking out at the moonlight shining on the sea and gentle waves lapping the shore. It was all so beautiful. Evan came in a few minutes later. He came and stood by me and we looked out at the dark sea together. He put his arms round my shoulders and bent his head forward.

"Susannah, my love."

I turned to face him and he kissed my lips, my face and my neck. His hands travelled down my body and my fears melted away. It seemed I wanted him as much as he wanted me. He picked me up and carried me to the bed. I averted my eyes modestly while he undressed and then he came and lay beside me. I had thought I would be shy but as he undressed me I just wanted to give myself to him. His caresses became more passionate until finally we came together. Briefly there was pain but then more passion and we became as one. This was what we had waited for and it had been worth it. When I awoke next morning it was such a joy to have him lying beside me. I watched him as he slept, his wavy mid brown hair, his silky moustache. His eyelids fluttered and he said, "I know you are watching me."

"Ah, you've caught me out then."

"Could we manage a little kiss this early in the day?"

He didn't wait for an answer but suddenly grabbed me and enfolded me with his arms and the little kiss became much, much more.

We laughed and we loved and those few days in Weston were filled with great tenderness. As Evan had said it certainly was a new world for us; a world I hadn't known existed; a world we were both more than happy to venture into. At the end of the week we had to go back into the real world where Evan went to work in the Jewellery Quarter every morning while I kept house, cooked meals and did the washing. He came home every evening and swept me off my feet. How blest I was.

The wedding photo was proudly displayed on the dresser. My bouquet, as I had expected, was faded but I took a few flowers and pressed them between sheets of tissue paper to dry and preserve them. I carefully wound the blue ribbon round my fingers to keep it as flat as possible and found a strong wooden box to keep my treasures in and carefully laid the flowers and the ribbon in the bottom of it.

My lovely new mother–in-law, Sarah, was living just next door. After those afternoons of sewing and chatting with her before the wedding I came to love her and regard her as my friend.

Chapter Six

Sarah from Wales

In the weeks before my eldest son Evan and dear Susannah were married she would sometimes come round from where she was living with Florence Smith in Birchfield Road and bring her sewing. We would sit in front of the fire and have a good chat. My dear Charley often calls me a chatterbox, but Susannah seemed quite content to sit and listen to me

From the moment Evan first brought her home I knew there was some unhappiness somewhere in her life. There was a reserve about her which spoke of some event, maybe in her childhood that had prevented her from being as happy as she might have been. When she smiled they were just fleeting smiles. I could see Evan adored her and was protective towards her and gradually she smiled more and became more relaxed.

Then of course there was the dreadful time when, due to her father's dismissal from the police force, she lost her teaching position so I began to know more about her and to realise that throughout her childhood he had been a problem. Eventually she told me about her mother's childhood in the workhouse but this was deemed to be an embarrassment so we didn't dwell on it. God knows how destitute people even today dread being sent to the workhouse for it really is the lowest thing that can happen to you; so no wonder Mary Hall, Susannah's mother, avoided mentioning it.

Susannah said, "The education my mother received there made her determined to rise above her early misfortunes and to do her best by her family. I'm afraid my father did not help her cause at all."

"Rather discouraging wasn't it?" I added.

"Yes it was. Mother was very proud of me when I became a teacher but it was a blow to her as well as to me when that finished. Anyway the time I spent with the Robertson's was very interesting and now we're preparing for the wedding so it's a very happy, exciting time."

"And dear Susannah, it's a great joy to me that you and Evan will be living next door to us and that as your family grows I will see them grow up and be close to them."

So those afternoons before they were married at Easter 1890 were very pleasurable to both of us and I became very fond of her. As I said I'm quite a chatterbox and I enjoyed re-living my memories when I told her about my early years. I told her about my childhood in Kerry in Montgomeryshire where I was born in 1836 and where my father was a farmer and miller. I told her how when I was a little girl my mother, also Sarah, had taken me back to her childhood home on the slopes of the Long Mynd at Myndtown where her brother Thomas was living with his wife and family and rearing sheep on the hills much as his father, another Thomas, had done before him.

"Susannah it was such a wonderful place where the gorse covered hill rose up steeply behind the farmhouse and the drovers' road twisted and turned upwards, where the sheep were grazing and the larks rose up singing from the sheep

16. Kerry Church interior

17. Near Bahaillion Bank

bitten turf. I remember my grandmother, Ann Howells, as

a very old lady, sitting by the fire with a shawl round her shoulders rocking the cradles of successive babies."

"Why ever did you leave such a beautiful place?"

"Well everything changed as my father died when I was eighteen. We'd had a relatively prosperous although hardworking life at Penygelli Mill and before that at Goitre Mill at Kerry. My mother, with the help of my brother Thomas, carried on running the mill for some years. She was still there when she was seventy-five but gradually she went blind and eventually went to live with my sister Jane at Bahaithlon Hamlet high up on the hills above Sarn. She died when she was eighty-five and was buried in Sarn Churchyard. I remember the views from Jane's home; on a clear day you could see right over to the mountain called Cader Idris, not that Mam could see that unfortunately.

18. Penygelli Mill
Photo courtesy of Richard Voice

My sister Mary married Edward Benbow two years after

my father died and went to live in Oswestry in Shropshire but most of my brothers and sisters stayed near Kerry. There didn't seem to be room for me any longer after my father died, and anyway I had a spirit of adventure and needed to earn my living. Now that the railway had been built as far as Craven Arms I realised I could go into the wider world to find work. So bidding my family a fond farewell I packed up my bundle, jumped on the carriers cart and caught the train from Craven Arms to Shrewsbury and hence onward to Birmingham."

"I think you were very adventurous going off on your own like that but you must have missed your family."

"Yes you're right, I did but I think the excitement of my new life helped me to get over my Da's death. There was plenty of work for housemaids and I soon found a position at the home of a Mrs Parker at one of the big houses in the Jewellery Quarter. I think you've probably been up that way with Evan?"

"Yes, I have. It was when we went to his workshop to talk about the lovely engagement ring he was going to make for me." And she looked down at her left hand and proudly touched her ring.

"It's not the same there now." I added thoughtfully, "I think the garden has been built over for yet more workshops but it was pleasant twenty-five to thirty years ago especially in the square around St Paul's Church."

"Is that where you met Evan's father?"

"Well yes it was. One day I just happened to smile at the

gardener's boy. Then it wasn't long before he was making any excuse he could to call at the kitchen door asking about what vegetables we were wanting or telling me it was likely to rain on the washing.

One day in the spring he got round to asking me when my afternoon off was. And there he was at the door, waiting for me with a gardenia from the glasshouse to pin to my hat."

"Good afternoon Miss Sarah," he said raising his cap to me, "how about a turn round the Square?"

"He indicated that I should take his arm and he looked as if the cat had got the cream. Then we were off, me with my arm tucked into his. I think it was almost love at first sight really. We couldn't stop stealing glances at each other and blushing and giggling.

We'd hoped for many afternoons spent strolling round the square and further afield but the incessant rain in the summer of 1860 put paid to that. So what were we to do? Usually housemaids were discouraged from having a follower in the house but as a special concession given the weather that year was among the coldest and wettest it had been for many years Mrs Parker allowed us to sit in the kitchen on my afternoon off."

"Mind you behave yourselves though," she said, "I don't want any hanky panky going on. You can get on with the mending Sarah."

"Maybe she thought that as I was twenty-three and Charley a year older we were not such giddy young things as some maids and gardeners boys might be. Little did she know! Many an afternoon when Charley came for me he'd look at the sky and say, "

"It's a bit black o'er Bill's mother's so can we sit by the fire instead of going out, me duck? We'll just get drenched again." So that's what we did. And I got on with the mending in case Mrs Parker came down stairs to see what we were up to. "Come on me duck," he'd say after a bit, "come and sit on me lap and we can have a bit of a cuddle."

"So I did and it was really nice. He'd kiss the side of my neck and I got tingles all up and down my back. He stroked my shoulder and then his hand started to move across my bodice. We kissed and his hand started fondling my breasts. But it wouldn't do. I jumped up, 'Charley Voice you just stop that at once. What if Mrs Parker comes downstairs?' I exclaimed. So I went and sat doing the mending again, all innocent like."

"You were lucky she allowed him to come into the house otherwise your romance might not have flourished," Susannah said.

"Yes, you're right, we were lucky. So the weeks went by and often I sat on his lap for a bit and his kisses got more and more passionate and when it was time for him to go we embraced each other and I realised how aroused he was. In May the family went away to Buxton Spa for a week leaving me and the other housemaid to give the house a good spring clean. So every day it was beating carpets, polishing floors, taking curtains down, cleaning the silver, on and on endlessly or there'd be ructions when

Madam came back. You know what it's like Susannah as you have been in that position yourself. But I still had my afternoon off and still it rained and still Charley came into the kitchen. 'Remember Charley, Mrs Parker said again 'no hanky panky' before she went away,' I said wagging my finger at him. 'Oh Sarah I really need some hanky panky,' he said as he grabbed hold of me and held me against him for a long passionate kiss.''

At this point Susannah who had been sitting quietly on the other side of the fireplace, started blushing and no doubt realised what I was leading up to. So I had to keep my memories to myself of what exactly happened next but it made me happy to remember how we had loved each other, how we had kissed and held each other and how we had continued to love each other all through the years. ''Nevertheless that afternoon in May was a turning point because a few weeks later I realised I'd fallen pregnant. I didn't know how I was going to tell Charley or what he'd do. Would he go off and leave me in the lurch as many chaps did when they got a girl in the family way? 'You silly ninny,' he'd said as he put his arms round me, 'there's nothing I'd like better than to marry you and start a family. So there!' Then he made me laugh through my tears when he got down on one knee in front of me and with such a solemn look on his face said,

'Miss Sarah Watkin will you do me the honour of becoming my wife?'

'Oh you daft ha'penny, of course I will!' I'd replied''

Over on the other side of the table Susannah allowed herself to smile.

"In October we were married at St Martin's in the Bull Ring in Birmingham and my pregnancy was plain to see My mother, who by then was beginning to lose her sight, felt she could not make the journey and stayed in Shrewsbury where she was living for a while with my sister Ann. But Charley's parents, John and Sarah, were there, having come in on the train from Castle Bromwich six miles away. We would be going back with them to Castle Bromwich for a cottage was waiting there for us and a job for Charley."

19. Cottages at Castle Bromwich
Photo courtesy of Richard Voice

"I've been into that church at the bottom of the Bull Ring. It's in a very busy part of town isn't it?" Susannah said.

"Yes it is and when we emerged as a married couple into the crowds of shoppers I said to Charley, 'I just know it's all going to work out all right. You've got yourself a gardening job and we've got a little cottage to move into.

What could be better than that?' 'Oh just that the general stores is next door so you won't have far to go if you run out of anything.' He'd said with a grin."

"It sounds perfect for your first home," Susannah added.

"Yes it was and we were happy living in that little cottage in Castle Bromwich. Just down the village street were the shoemaker, two dressmakers, a carpenter, farm workers, a carter and a farmer who was a butcher as well. Our friend John Cooper was the innkeeper at the Castle Inn. A little further away were the blacksmiths and the tollgate, this being an important coaching route between London and Chester. As well as the Castle Inn there were two other taverns to supply the needs of travellers who wanted a quick bite to eat and a place to change the horses. One was the Bradford Arms, named for Lord Bradford whose family had owned the Castle Bromwich Hall for generations and the other was the Coach and Horses on the Green."

"How far away did his parents live?"

"Oh not far and there was a well-trodden path between that hostelry and our cottage for Charley's parents lived next door to it. Their cottage was overflowing with family members for in addition to Charley's brother John there was Elizabeth, his married sister, her husband Thomas Riley and their four children. The good standing of the family in the village must have helped Charley get the job of being coachman and gardener to Mr John Bateman, the architect who lived at Hawkeshead House. His son Charles, who also became a well-known architect of many buildings in Birmingham, was born in the same year as our daughter Matilda.

While we lived there three of our children were born. Evan arrived in the February after we were married. It was hard having a new baby in a tiny cottage so early in the year. Trying to keep the place warm at the tail end of the winter was no easy task. In rural areas about half of the children of farm labourers, artisans and servants died before they were five and many of those were babies in their first year of life. But Evan survived and two years later Matilda was born and then Thomas in 1865. By this time the tiny village cottage was bursting at the seams and we began to look for somewhere else to live."

Susannah said, "I remember the two cottages where we lived in Worcestershire being very crowded when all the children were small."

I went on, "Charley had a good reference from Mr Bateman and found employment as a gardener and coachman in the area of Handsworth known as Handsworth Wood. This was where wealthy people who owned businesses in Birmingham were building themselves large houses surrounded by spacious grounds with stabling and coach houses. In fact now I would say about five times as many people live here as did fifty years ago. There was no house with this new job but with the increase in his wages we were able to rent one of this pair of newly built semi-detached cottages in Wellington Road and here we still are today.

Charley had been well placed to find employment. His gardening skills had been praised by Mr Bateman as the spacious grounds of his house had been maintained beautifully and enhanced with spring bulbs, roses for the summer and many lovely shrubs which flowered at different times of the year, making sure there was always something of interest to see in the garden. Being able to handle a pair of carriage horses was a skill he had acquired from an early age when he lived next door to 'The Coach and Horses' and had worked with the horses in the stables there. So the work he found as gardener and coachman was ideal for him."

"I can just imagine how beautiful that garden must have been," Susannah mused, "having grown accustomed to the Robertsons' lovely garden."

"Yes it was and throughout the year too. Anyway, sorry though we were to leave Castle Bromwich and all our friends and neighbours we were delighted to move into this house that actually has a flushing water closet just across a porch by the back door instead of a privy at the end of the garden and that has a cold water tap and a sink in the scullery instead of a pump outside shared by four cottages. We felt we were moving into the modern world. You know Susannah all this talking is making my throat dry. I'm going to put the kettle on." So I got up and walked into the scullery to fill the kettle from the tap there. Susannah felt like stretching her legs and followed me through the doorway.

"As you can see the scullery here also has the luxury of a copper boiler in the corner with a fire underneath it where not only is water for washing the clothes heated but also hot water for the weekly bath. We still bring the tin tub in from its place in the outhouse and put in front of the kitchen range. The tap on the front of the copper boiler is turned on allowing water to flow into large enamel jugs from which the water is poured into the bath. One by one we all have our bath starting with the girls and me first and then after that the men of the family. I know that wealthy people have a bath every day in a proper bathroom but when I think of the palaver we have to go through to have a bath once a week I feel that is quite enough."

I carried the kettle back into the other room and put it on the hob to boil while we settled back down again to resume our chat.

"Over the years Charley has made a beautiful garden at the side of the cottage for us, where as you know he grows vegetables and flowers and there are lavender hedges to attract the bees and butterflies too. Lizzie was born here in 1871 and then Alice four years later but in 1878 tragedy befell my sister Mary in Oswestry when her husband Edward died. Her eldest daughter Jessie was twenty at the time and she came here to Birmingham and became a housemaid just as I had done twenty years earlier. Although she had a live in position she often came to see us and I was very fond of her.

Three years later she fell for a young man and they let their passion run away with them and she became pregnant. However, unlike my dear Charley, the fellow concerned left her in the lurch and she came to me with a tale of great woe. There was no question of letting her go to the workhouse to have her baby and she couldn't go back home to her mother who had enough troubles of her own coping with seven children and no husband. So she had the baby here in this house and here he stayed and Jessie was free to continue with her life. He was a sweet baby and Jessie named him Edward Harold. And that is the story of dear Harry who has become a son to us and whom we have always loved just as much as our other children. But thinking back to the days when we lived in Castle Bromwich, Evan went to the tiny school in the village at first."

"I saw it when he took me to see Castle Bromwich."

"Oh yes I heard you'd had a nice trip over there on the train and had been to see Charley's brother and his wife as well. Anyway by the time we'd moved to Handsworth, Tilly had reached school age so they went together to the nearby school next to St Mary's Church. Evan found the school very different from the village school. The teachers were very strict and the classes were large. Morning school began with religious education and the teaching for the rest of the day concentrated on Reading, Writing and Arithmetic. The children wrote on slates with a slate pencil. After the teacher had marked the work it was rubbed out with a damp rag or a bit of spit and finished off with a coat sleeve. But of course Susannah this is all familiar to you from your time as a teacher isn't it?"

"Yes indeed it is and what you are saying brings back some memories for me not only of when I was teaching but from when I was a pupil myself. And also every day there would have been drill in the school yard when it was fine and in the school hall when it was wet. All the children stood in straight rows and their movements had to be synchronised."

"The years passed and eventually all the children went to school." I continued, "I did some work as a laundress to bring in some much needed extra money. Evan and Thomas became jewellers. Tilly went into service and now is a laundry maid at Combermere Abby in Cheshire. Like me when I was young, she has spread her wings and gone far away. However returning for visits is much easier by now for the railways are everywhere. Lizzie joined me with the laundry work and Alice takes in dressmaking so now Harry at ten years old is the only one still at school. Talking of him reminds me, just look at the clock. He'll be in from school any minute and wanting a bite to eat so I'll have to stop my chattering. Oh look, Susannah! We forgot about having that cup of tea after all."

So my afternoons with Susannah passed happily and usefully as we prepared for her wedding to my dear son Evan at Easter 1890.

Chapter Seven

Married Life 1890-1904

Susannah's mother Mary takes up the story:

It is with great nostalgia that I remember that happy wedding day fourteen years ago and the pleasant months afterwards when the newlyweds settled into their home and their life together. I had never before seen Susannah so carefree and joyful. She loved having her own home to look after and she enjoyed preparing meals that she and Evan would share in the evening when he returned from work. She continued to make curtains and rag rugs to brighten up the rooms and she polished the furniture with beeswax polish until you could see your face in it. She arranged flowers from the garden and made the house look most attractive.

All through the ensuing years we spent an afternoon together at least once a week when we would sit in front of the fire when it was cold and do our mending together. And we would chat.

From time to time Evan's mother came in to join us. But usually she was busy as she still had Harry at school. Sometimes Annie came over with her baby Charles Thomas and she proudly showed off his latest developments. As the years passed there were days of happiness and laughter and days of sadness when tears were shed. But in those first months there was just happiness and soon Susannah was looking forward to giving birth to her first baby. Evan's father made a crib with rockers on it and we sat and sewed baby clothes and I made a pretty quilt for the crib. Every evening Evan came home and kissed Susannah and asked her how her day had gone and if she was feeling well.

Through that winter Evan had been coughing as he usually did in the winter and the doctor said he had asthma and bronchitis. We knew that his small, cold and dusty workshop where he created beautiful diamond rings wasn't helping him at all. In the spring thankfully he recovered as usual. By early March the days had lengthened and winter was behind us at last. Evan's father had taken over and improved the neglected garden as neither Susannah nor Evan were able to deal with it and so, as he was living next door, it just became one large garden where he grew vegetables for both families and also some flowers. There were hens near the bottom of the garden too so there were always fresh eggs and fresh vegetables for both households and even some for me sometimes.

On the day that Susannah went into labour a lovely bunch of bright daffodils had been brought in to go on the table. When she felt her pains starting she went next door to Evan's Mam.

"Mam, my pains have started. Can you send Harry for my Ma?"

"Yes, he's just come in so I'll send him off straight away. Now don't you worry about anything my love. It's your first baby so you've plenty of time and your ma will be here soon. Just you sit down here and I'll make us both a cup of tea when I've sent Harry on his way to Warstone Lane."

By the time I got there Susannah was walking up and down restlessly and when her pains came on she leaned against the wall or over a chair and shut her eyes until the pain had passed. As it was her first baby we were expecting her to be in labour for many hours and she was. When the pains became bad she went to her bed and I sat with her. It was now forty years since Queen Victoria had used chloroform to dull the pain of childbirth but on this occasion Susannah did without it. She lay there trying so hard not to make a fuss as the contractions became stronger. Evan came back from work and sat with her for a while but eventually when she started moaning and crying out she sent him back down stairs where he paced backwards and forwards or went out into the garden where he could not hear what was going on upstairs. The midwife came and Evan's mother and I were with her when finally two hours later little Sidney was born. I called downstairs,

"It's a boy and you can come up in five minutes to see your son."

When we'd tidied her up Evan came to join us upstairs. The joy on his face was a delight to see as he cradled his tiny son but it was to his beloved Susannah that he gave his main attention. "My poor darling," he said as he bent over her and tenderly kissed her.

"We have a son Evan, isn't he sweet?"

"He's amazing. Look at his tiny fingers, he's holding on to me already."

At that moment little Sidney let out a lusty cry and I said,

"He's telling us he's hungry so put him to the breast Susannah and see if he knows how to suck."

Sidney soon found out how to get the milk and when he had fed he settled down to a good sleep and so did Susannah for she was exhausted, poor dear. Sidney Howard was christened at St Mary's, Handsworth on Sunday 12th April and as Thomas and Annie's son Charles Thomas had not yet been christened it was decided that it would be good to have both babies christened on the same day. The Voyce, Hall and Hawker families gathered at the church in the afternoon for the ceremony. By that time Charles Thomas was a year old and was almost walking. These babies were the first of many grandchildren for Sarah and Charles Voice. Thomas and Annie had seven more children; Tilly and her husband Richard Briggs in Yorkshire had Charles in 1899, Horace in 1903 and William in 1904. Their only daughter Alice was born in 1901. Evan's sister Alice married Daniel Dolan and their daughter was named Winifred.

Susannah and Annie met often and enjoyed watching each other's babies learning to smile, crawl, walk and play together. And soon there was another wedding to plan because Evan's sister Lizzie was marrying Henry Hurst at Trinity Church, Birchfields in March. For Susannah and Annie there were memories of their own weddings in the same church two years previously

By the time of Lizzie's wedding to Henry Susannah knew that she was pregnant again. During her first pregnancy she had felt well but this time she felt more tired and was relieved when I offered to take Sidney off her hands for a few hours two or three times a week. She went into labour on the first of August and I remember telling her, "This is your second baby so you won't be in so much pain." I couldn't have been more wrong.

She was in agony and despite trying to push that baby out into the world it just would not come. Two days of moaning and screaming went by and she was becoming exhausted and too weak to push. Evan was beside himself with worry. He couldn't bear to think of his beloved wife suffering so badly. Although I barely remembered my mother I knew she had died in childbirth and was so afraid that we were going to lose Susannah in the same way. Despite the expense we had to send for the doctor.

"This couldn't have gone on much longer. It may be too late already." He said. "This baby has an abnormally large head. In order to deliver it I shall have to use forceps and I shall administer chloroform so the mother will not suffer any more."

The drops of chloroform were sprinkled on a cloth and held to her face until she became unconscious. The screaming ceased. The doctor did his work as quickly and carefully as possible but it was a brutal procedure. Finally, the baby, a girl, was delivered and as the doctor had foretold the child's head was very large. He warned Evan that she might not develop properly and that it was likely that she would only live for a few months.

"And what about my wife?" Evan wanted to know.

"I'm afraid she has suffered a great deal," the doctor told him, "whether or not she gets over it only time will tell."

217

Evan turned his face away so that I would not see the extreme anguish that he suffered. "Oh my God," he said, "not my wife, not my poor wife." He sat on a chair by Susannah's bed and held his head in his hands. "Susannah, don't leave me, I couldn't bear it."

I looked at the still, white faced form on the bed and thought that she very possibly could drift away. Death was lurking near to us that day but did not take Susannah from us. When she regained consciousness she wanted to see the baby but could tell from the look on Evan's face that all was not well. He picked his tiny deformed daughter up from the crib carefully and held her out to Susannah. "Her head is overlarge, there is something wrong with her. This is why you had such a terrible time giving birth to her."

He spared Susannah the details about the baby's life expectancy at that point but as she gradually recovered she learnt that this little girl would not be a normal child and that she had fluid on the brain. Two weeks later on 24th August Susannah was well enough to leave the house leaning on Evan's arm and the baby was christened Ethel at St Mary's Church, Handsworth.

The doctor had been right that baby Ethel would not live long. Her short life ended seventeen months later on January 2nd 1894 and what a nightmare those months were for the whole family. Sidney was nearly three at the time of Ethel's death so he was himself hardly out of babyhood. He was toddling around by then and learning to talk and getting into everything as toddlers do. Ethel cried continuously and was a problem to feed. Susannah and Evan both looked strained from lack of sleep. Ethel's head became more and more enlarged as the fluid in her head accumulated. She never learned to sit up or crawl like a normal child and when I held her in my arms her large head lolled to one side. I will never forget the sight of Evan cradling his screaming daughter with tears running down his face, "I don't know what to do with her, poor little mite," he said to me. "She's in terrible pain. I wish the Lord would take her so her suffering ends."

That last winter was a grim time. Evan, as usual in the winter, was suffering from bronchitis and Susannah suffered badly from morning sickness. She was pregnant again and worried stiff that the next birth would be a repeat of the last one. I sometimes wondered why she still allowed Evan to make love to her knowing what the consequences would be but they adored each other and she would do anything for him. And just now they both needed the love and comfort they could give to each other.

Evan's mother and I did as much as we could to help and would take Sidney off her hands for a while most days. Annie also came round frequently but she'd had another baby, John Clarence, two months after Ethel was born and, like Susannah, was also expecting again. So when poor little Ethel died on January 2nd there was a certain amount of relief mixed in with the sadness. Later the same day Evan left the house with a grim face as he went off to register the death. When he returned home Susannah held on to him and wept. "This is the help and comfort we promised to give each other when we were married," she said through her tears. "Oh Evan I'm so afraid about giving birth next time. Look, I'm so huge already and this baby isn't due until March."

But when she went into labour in March the doctor was on hand with the chloroform for the birth and it was very helpful. Susannah was safely delivered of twins, a boy and a girl. So what had happened with poor Ethel was fortunately not repeated. The babies, born on March 21st were taken to St Mary's Church to be christened Florry and Harry on 8th April. Florry grew to be a strong sturdy little girl who loved looking after everybody and through the following years there was going to be much need of that. Evan adored her and as soon as she could walk she brought his slippers to him in the evening when he returned from work and would often sit on his knee and chatter to him. She helped more than anyone else to numb the pain of Ethel's short life. Every mother expects to lose one or more babies and so it was with Susannah. Harry was the weaker twin and did not thrive. He died in infancy.

One day in 1895 when I went to see her Susannah held out the newspaper for me to see. "Look Ma," she said, "There's an article here about Dr Dale who has just died."

"So who was Dr Dale?" I said as I took my coat off.

"Don't you remember? I told you about him when I was living with Florence. He was the preacher at Carrs Lane Church. I used to go there sometimes with her. He used to preach very memorable sermons about the causes of poverty and how to improve living conditions. He said Christians should spread the word of God by living it. He was a great man."

There was also another death in 1895 and that was of my brother John who lived at Tipton. I was sad to see him go and well-remembered how, over fifty years earlier, he had to become head of the family when our parents died in the early 1840s in Hereford. He'd had the anguish of seeing his four younger sisters go into the workhouse when they were very young, the loss of his first wife and baby son, the tragedy of Catherine's death by drowning in the canal with the horror of going out and searching for her body and then of course the family disgrace of Jane's prison sentence and the disapproval of the unsavoury company she'd kept. So he'd seen more than his share of sadness in his time.

It wasn't long before Susannah was pregnant again and in 1896 Walter Charles was born on March 17th. He was christened at St Mary's Handsworth on 10th April. From the start Susannah adored him and without a doubt he was always her favourite child. His birth had been the easiest of them all and by now the nightmare of Ethel's birth and the memory of her short life was beginning to fade away.

Sidney had probably suffered just as much as Evan and Susannah during that difficult time. With Ethel needing constant attention from her weary parents, Sidney probably felt unloved but help was at hand in the form of Evan's father to whom he became very attached. By the time he was five he could often be seen helping Grandpa in the garden and with the chickens and had been given the special job of egg collecting. When I went to see them Sidney would take my hand and lead me down to the hen house and show me the warm brown eggs he was collecting. "Grandma, when the hens cackle I know there is another egg." He showed me his part of the garden with pride and pointed out the carrots, potatoes and lettuces he was growing.

"He's going to be a grand gardener." Charley said, "He's got a real feel for it."

"Well that's useful," I replied. "He'll stop us going hungry."

The next year, 1897, was a year of great celebration for us all as it was the Diamond Jubilee of our dear Queen Victoria. On Sunday 20th June we all went to church where the hymn 'King of Kings' specially composed for the occasion was sung at all the churches in the land. Tuesday the 22nd June was declared a public holiday and there were many bonfires on hills throughout the country. Susannah reminded me of when Her Majesty had visited Birmingham ten years earlier and she had gone with Evan's Mam, Harry and Alice to see her in town.

One day in November when I went round to Susannah's Sidney was full of excitement. "Grandpa and Pa are taking me to Bingley Hall tomorrow."

"And what are you going to see there me duck?"

"There are going to be bands playing and a troupe of dancers and clowns."

Supporting Walter on one hip Susannah used her spare hand to push The Birmingham Daily Post across the table for me to see.

"Here's the paper Ma. Look, it says 'Birmingham Great Victorian Diamond Jubilee Chrysanthemum Exhibition, today and tomorrow 11th November, lighted by new intensified gaslight.' As Sidney has told you there will be bands and dancers and goodness knows what. He'll love it and Grandpa will enjoy the flowers as well. Admission between ten in the morning and three o'clock one shilling, and sixpence for the rest of the day."

"Well I know Charley has a passion for Chrysanths and the rest of it looks as if it will be fun as well."

When I went round the following week Sidney was marching up and down the garden being a drummer, or so he thought. And Charley was thumbing through a catalogue of Chrysanthemums. I gathered the trip had been a great success.

During the Autumn Sidney harvested his carrots and proudly dug up the potatoes he had grown in the garden. He loved pottering about out there, plying Charley with questions. Charley was fond of his company. Florry and Sidney loved to go next door to their Welsh grandmother who would tell stories of her own childhood in Wales and about Ann, their great, great grandmother at the farm on the slopes of the Long Mynd in Shropshire.

That Christmas it was decided that some of the older children in Evan and Thomas's families were old enough for a trip to the pantomime. On the first Monday after Christmas there was a performance of Aladdin at 2pm at the Grand Theatre, situated in Corporation Street overlooking Old Square. Florry at the age of three wasn't really old enough to go but Evan took Sidney and Alice's Winifred and Thomas took his Charles Thomas and Jack. At sixteen irrepressible Harry decided that he was still young enough to go so off they all went. When they came back after the performance Harry was full of it as usual.

"Susannah you wouldn't believe the size of the place. It seats over two thousand people and is beautifully done out in crimson and gold with velvet curtains."

"I loved the dancing by the celebrated Carlos Troupe." Winifred added.

"There was lots of singing from the chorus too, and actors and the genie of the lamp."

"And Aladdin had the magic ring so was able to overcome whatever the wicked sorcerer did."

"Not forgetting the comedian and writer of the show, Mr Percy Milton."

They'd all had a good time and followed with a good Boxing Day tea with all of us round the table Christmas 1897 came to a close.

Meanwhile far away in Africa there was rising unrest which was eventually going to have repercussions on the family in Wellington Road and my family in Hockley. We read in the newspapers that after the British had taken over Cape Colony from the Dutch at the end of the 1700s they had insisted that only English should be spoken and that this caused much resentment among the Dutch settlers, who in 1830 had set up the new states of the Transvaal and the Orange Free State; there was a great trek northwards by the 'Voortrekkers' to the new states.

Later, with the discovery of gold and diamonds, the British again wanted to expand their empire northwards. The 'Uitlanders', many of whom were British, who had swelled the population of the areas when they went there to mine the gold and diamonds, became dissatisfied that they had no say in the politics of the area. Sir Joseph Chamberlain, well known to the residents of Birmingham was now the British Colonial Secretary and with the British High Commissioner in South Africa, Sir Alfred Milner, believed the Transvaal was pressing for a United South Africa under the Afrikaners. Milner felt that war would be the only way to stop the Boers threatening British supremacy.

To Sarah's dismay, Harry, always impulsive and searching for adventure, suddenly announced, "I've enlisted in the Coldstream Guards Mam. Joseph Chamberlain is calling for us to be patriotic. He's a good chap. Look what he's done for Birmingham so I'm going to do my bit for Queen and country."

"Oh Harry do think things over a bit more before you take these rash decisions. It's so far away. We won't know what's happening to you."

"I'll write Mam and you'll be able to read all about it in the newspapers."

Nothing would dissuade him from his thirst for adventure and he sailed for Africa in September 1899. he was eighteen years old. In his first short letter home he spoke of the boredom of the long boat journey with so little to do as the days stretched out and how he couldn't wait to get out there and see some action. That was soon to come as the war broke out on 11th October that year.

During the day Susannah sometimes went next door to read Charley's paper, 'The Morning Post'. Sarah leaned over his shoulder and listened as he read the reports of the war some of which were written by a young correspondent called Winston Churchill who had daringly escaped after the Boers had captured him and then continued to write about his experiences as well as writing reports of the war. But they hadn't heard from Harry since that first letter. "Mind you, I'm not surprised," Sarah said, "when he was at school he had a struggle to string two words together when he was asked to write anything."

In the evenings Evan brought home the Birmingham Mail with yet more news of the war including reports on the sieges of Kimberly and Ladysmith. All the papers stirred up a tremendous feeling of jingoism and patriotism in the British people. "It's amazing that we can now hear the reports of the war within a day or two of the action thanks to the modern telegraph system." Susannah said.

"Yes," Evan replied, "this is the first war where that has happened. It's another example of the changes in our daily lives. Although I think we must realise that the papers are only putting the British point of view. Bearing in mind that the Boers are of Dutch descent we must realise that in Holland and Germany a very different point of view is being printed!"

"Oh dear, look, they're calling this Black Week." Charley said in the middle of December. "It's because the Boers have won impressive victories at places called Stromberg, Magersfontain and Colenso."

In January there was another victory for the Boers at Spionkop and still we didn't know if these were places where Harry was fighting or not. It was very worrying. But the tide changed and by late February Kimberley and Ladysmith had been relieved. On 13th March Lord Roberts, the British Commander in chief occupied Bloemfontein. There was great joy in Britain when news came through of the relief of Mafeking on 17th May, making Colonel Robert Baden-Powell, commander of the garrison there, an instant hero throughout the British Empire. On 5th June 1900 Lord Roberts took Pretoria.

Sarah didn't expect very detailed letters from her son but a few scribbled lines arrived from time to time and together with newspaper reports we gathered that the Coldstream Guards had not fought to relieve Kimberly or Mafeking but they had been at the battle of Modder River where there were four hundred and fifty British casualties compared with the seventy-five suffered by the Boer; we just hoped that Harry wasn't one of them. They had also spent much time marching about South Africa guarding military installations and supply trains.

On Friday 28thSeptember Evan and Susannah went to the Curzon Hall in Suffolk Street to see animated pictures of the Boer War, sitting in the mid-priced seats of one shilling and sixpence. The show was enhanced with Dyson's Diorama and Gypsy Choir. The previous night the pictures had been of 'Bonnie Scotland'. "Rather different from the African veldt," Evan remarked.

"Amazing to see what's happening out there, "Susannah added.

Although victory seemed at this point to be assured there was a recovery of the Boer resistance and there were surprise attacks on Lord Robert's supply lines. The Boers were able to quickly gather their commandos together, attack and then disappear, as if into thin air, in the terrain they knew so well. This phase of the war continued for another two years but by 1901 Harry was back at the Coldstream Guard Barracks in Hanover Square, London, announcing his arrival back in England by telegram. When eventually a lean and sun-tanned Harry came home there was jubilation in Wellington Road. Sarah couldn't take her eyes off him.

"Oh but it's good to see you again son." She said as she stretched up to give the tall, bronzed soldier a big hug. While Sarah and Susannah prepared a welcome home feast the men of the family gathered round him to hear his tales of battle and of marching across the veldt under the relentless sun. But when he told us of the events that he had seen before he left South Africa we became more concerned. In November 1900 Lord Herbert Kitchener had succeeded Lord Roberts who had come back to England.

"Those devilish Boers had started popping up all over the place, shooting us, derailing supply trains and causing no end of havoc just when we thought we had them licked." Harry said, "So Kitchener devised what came to be called a scorched earth policy. Thousands of square miles of farmland and Boer farms were burnt and salt was spread on the land so it couldn't be used for growing crops. Usually the men were away fighting but the women and children came out of those farms with their hands in the air. We herded them all up and took them to camps."

"We read something of that in the papers," Evan said. "I

suppose the women and children were safe away from the fighting."

"Well, no it wasn't quite like that," Harry added in a more serious voice than we were used to hearing from him, "because I'm afraid conditions were very bad in the camps and there was much disease and starvation. And then of course there were the deaths. It was pretty bad. I don't think the full extent of it was put in the papers. The whole idea of course was to deprive the fighters of food and supplies."

When his leave was over Harry went back to London and later that year we heard more about the horrors of the camps he had told us about. An amazing woman called Emily Hobhouse went to South Africa and visited some of the camps of which there were forty-five in total. She found extreme deprivation and cruelty which she revealed to a sceptical British public and an embarrassed government. The Fawcett Ladies Commission was set up. Further investigations revealed that twenty-eight thousand Boer women and children had died and at least twenty thousand black people had also lost their lives. This resulted in High Commissioner Lord Alfred Milner taking over the administration of the camps from the army. But it also brought about the end of the war as the Boers knew that under these conditions they could no longer continue to fight.

So for Evan, Susannah and their three surviving children the traumas of the early years of their marriage appeared to have settled down. Evan, as always, was bothered with bronchitis every winter but in the spring he recovered. He continued his work as a jeweller making many beautiful diamond rings but none of them were made with the love that had gone into the engagement ring he had made for Susannah.

As predicted the green fields of Handsworth gradually became covered with houses and the planners who had wanted Handsworth Park to be a green space for people to enjoy were proved right. On summer afternoons chairs were arranged round the bandstand and many a pleasant hour was spent enjoying the concerts.

The back-to-back houses of Hockley and other areas near to the town with their unsanitary living conditions continued to be a source of disease and the poverty of the people who lived there showed no signs of being alleviated. Children continued to have insufficient to eat while many parents spent what money there was on drowning their sorrows in drink. People scratched a living wherever they could and when they didn't have enough money to pay the rent they would do a moonlight flit. From where we lived in Warstone Lane you'd hear a handcart with their few possessions on board rumbling away through the streets during the hours of darkness.

The year 1901 brought great sadness to the nation when Queen Victoria died at Osborne House on the Isle of Wight on 22nd January. It also heralded a time of great sadness for my family. We moved from Warstone Lane to 110 Hockley Street in the heart of the Jewellery Quarter when our son John Thomas had become ill and was unable to work. He had married Clara in 1895 and their daughter Winifred was born the following year. Within a short time he had become very ill with consumption and was unable to carry on with his job as a jeweller's porter. It seemed sensible that we should move in with her and all try and rub along together as money was so tight.

Also living there were our daughter Mary Goode and her two children John Henry and William Bertram. Mary's husband, like Harold Voyce, was away fighting in the Boer War. So there were eight of us living in the house and one of them, my son John was very ill indeed. He spent his days sitting by the fire with his hacking cough and a spittoon by his side. He frequently coughed up blood. He looked like an old man but he was only thirty-two. For a mother to see her youngest son suffering so was very harrowing. It also brought back sad memories of my father Thomas suffering from tuberculosis so long ago in our impoverished dwelling in Hereford and then of him dying a few months later in the workhouse.

As 1900 drew to a close and the winter cold permeated the damp building John became much worse and finally took to his bed in the middle of January. Money was very tight but Will was still doing some work as a night watchman so the money he didn't spend down at the pub went towards the rent and feeding us all. It wasn't enough of course, so we three women took in washing and sewing, anything really to try to make ends meet. There was always damp washing, ours and other peoples, hanging around for it was difficult to dry it outside during the winter months.

Our eldest son William who was a carter lived in Little King Street not far away from us. He was able to bring us old wooden boxes, which we chopped up for firewood for ourselves and sometimes we sold bundles of it. We were better off than those folks living in the back to backs but only just. The wind whistled under the door and through the gaps where the windows didn't fit. To stop the draughts coming under the door we had a long 'sausage', a tube made out of some tough material and filled with rags.

The rain dripped from the blocked guttering, the chimney smoked and the fire gave out little heat. Trips to the privy down the yard were to be endured. It was a grim time. The children were all below school age and so with their colds and snivels were under our feet the whole time. At least with three women in the house even if one or two of them were out working there was always someone to keep an eye on the children but of course much of Clara's time was spent caring for her poor husband whose hacking cough never seemed to stop, poor man. He died on 23rd March and when I went with Clara to register his death two days later her eyes were red from crying.

No sooner had we begun to get over John Thomas's death than news came to us that our son Nimrod was in the Workhouse Infirmary also suffering from consumption. I know it was very common but to have two sons with it in one year seemed as if the odds were stacked against us. Nimrod had not been close to us through the years as he had joined the navy as a boy when he was sixteen and had travelled the world going to all parts of the British Empire. With him not being a prolific letter writer we'd had to be content with the occasional missive that arrived with an exotic stamp on it from far-flung parts of the Empire. As far as we knew he had never married. We never discussed it with him but perhaps he fitted the general picture of a sailor having a wife in every port, who knows? He'd come home to settle down a few years ago and was a general labourer but now this deadly disease had struck him down too. Although we all visited him when we could it was our eldest son William who was present at his death on the first of June and who went to register it on the fourth of June.

20. The Voyce Family c1902

There was further tragedy when Evan's sister Alice was widowed in the same year. "It couldn't get worse than this, could it?" I said to Susannah but for her it did before many more years were out. By this time William and I had twenty grandchildren so there were always two or three or more of them suffering from the childhood diseases of measles, whooping cough, scarlet fever and the rest. Illness was very much part of our lives as it was also of the people amongst whom we lived.

During the spring of 1903 Susannah became pregnant again. Since Walter's birth in 1896 their home life had been happy and settled although she had been much shaken to lose two of her brothers in 1901. She did whatever she could to comfort Alice who had moved back next door to be with her parents after she was widowed. And as usual we all worried each winter when Evan's bronchitis became much worse.

All the children were at school nearby and Susannah enjoyed seeing them learning to read and do their sums. She encouraged them to talk about their interests and when I went to visit them I thought what a lovely contented family they were. She and Evan were just as devoted as ever. Annie was very busy with her five sons and one daughter but she and Susannah met as often as they could to catch up on the news.

When Harry could spare the time he would come by train from London to visit Sarah and Charley and then drop by next door to regale the children with stories of the battles he had fought in Africa in the Boer War when he was in the Coldstream Guards. "And did you really see lions?" Sidney would ask, wide eyed with disbelief.

"Yes laddie and monkeys and black people and soldiers."

"I'm going to be a soldier when I grow up." Walter added

with confidence.

"Why have you stopped being a soldier?" Florry asked.

"The war is over, me duck, so I'm a policeman on the London to Brighton Railway now instead. If there is ever another war I'll soon be a soldier again."

My daughter Mary's husband, John Thomas Clifton Goode, also came safely back from the Boer War and had his photograph taken proudly showing his medals. But it was always a mystery to me that he had enlisted under a false name and although I tried to find out why he had done that I was never told the reason. Mary and her family moved away from Hockley Street to their own home in Pemberton Street and John Goode became a hardware packer. Edward Beale, a tailor, was courting John Thomas's widow Clara and we were hopeful that they might find happiness together. He was kind to her daughter Winifred.

Winter came and, although Susannah was heavily pregnant, Christmas was celebrated in style. A fir tree was placed in the front room and Evan and the children decorated it with painted fir cones and glittering ornaments. Secrets abounded and presents were wrapped and put under the tree to be opened after Christmas Dinner.

No one had much money but money doesn't buy happiness and everyone was happy as they gathered round the piano to sing carols on Christmas Eve. Seven-year-old Walter gazed at the tree in wonder as he sat on the floor by his mother's feet enjoying the carols while Florry helped her Pa with the music at the piano. Thirteen-year-old

21. John Thomas Clifton Goode 1865-1941
22. and below (circled) with his Regiment
Both photos courtesy of William Clark

Sidney was shy about singing because his voice was just beginning to break so he stood behind me where he hoped he wouldn't be noticed. Evan's Mam and Pa came round with Alice from next door and her fourteen-year-old daughter Winifred sat on the floor by Sarah's feet, her long blond hair catching the reflection of the candles on the mantelpiece. They all sat cosily together in the warmth while the flames in the hearth created flickering shadows on the wall. Outside the world was quiet and blanketed by crisp snow. The Voyce family were in a world of their own.

Suddenly there was a banging at the door, and Harry burst in, with snow on his cap, noisy and full of life as always and a firm favourite with all his nephews and nieces.

"We wish you a Merry Christmas,
  We wish you a Merry Christmas,
  We wish you a Merry Christmas and Happy New Year."
He sang.

All the children joined in with

"We all want some figgy pudding,
  We all want some figgy pudding,
  We all want some figgy pudding, so bring some out here."

It got faster and faster as we all joined in,

"We won't go until we've got some,
  We won't go until we've got some,
  We won't go until we've got some so bring some out here."

"Typical Harry," Sarah laughed, "Always causing a riot."

"Cocoa in the kitchen for the children and then to bed," ordered Evan amid cries of dismay but off they had to go. Evan's word was law.

Evan, Susannah and the children walked to church at St Mary's on Christmas morning with Lizzie and Henry while Sarah and Alice cooked a delicious lunch for as many of the Voyce family as could be there. On Boxing Day Susannah and her family came to us in Hockley Street and Mary and her family joined us, as did Clara and Winifred with Edward Beale. And the next day Christmas was over and it was back to work as normal. That Christmas we had visited each other's homes and shared mince pies and other seasonal treats. Carols were sung round the piano and for a while everyone forgot their poverty and sadness caused by the loss of loved ones. It was a happy interlude that the younger generation would look back on fondly in the years to come.

Susannah went into labour on 17th of January. It was a straightforward birth and her daughter Hetty was born the same day. She was a bonny baby and was much loved by her two brothers and her ten year old sister Florry. Indeed Florry's 'looking after people' skills came to the fore and she was quite a little mother to Hetty and enjoyed helping Susannah care for her. The baby was baptised at St Mary's Church on 10th February when once more the extended Voyce family gathered round the font.

It was worrying that winter that Evan's usual bout of bronchitis did not clear up as quickly as usual and during the summer his asthma attacks were worse than they had previously been By late summer Hetty was developing well. Her blonde hair was long enough to be tied back with ribbons and when the family photograph was taken in the garden on a fine day in the early autumn she was sitting on Susannah's lap and wearing her first pair of shoes. Both the girls were wearing their best white dresses and looked very pretty. Dear little Walter, everyone's favourite, stood next to his mother with Sidney behind him. Sidney had now left school and started work as a gardener's boy so he was proud to be contributing to the family finances. Evan completed the group and afterwards we realised that by then he was already looking gaunt compared with a photograph that had been taken two years previously when he had been very upright and more smartly dressed.

Susannah was very busy with her family as usual during that autumn. Every morning Evan and Sidney went off to work with a packet of bread and cheese and sometimes a pickled onion. Florry and Walter went to school and that left Susannah at home with Hetty. Hetty was almost walking and was getting in to everything and chattered away to Susannah in words that only she knew the meaning of. She was a charming baby. I continued to go to Susannah's at least once a week but with running my own home and visiting my other daughter Mary and her children my days were busy and my old legs were beginning to play me up. I realised now I was sixty-seven that the years were catching up with me. I'd had a hard life so it wasn't really surprising that I was feeling old.

Early in the year Clara and Edward Beale were married and their daughter Beatrice was born at the beginning of the winter. It was good to know that she had a husband again

Evan's mother and Susannah, living next door to each other, were very close but like me Sarah also had other grandchildren that took up her time.

23. The Voyce family, possibly with Hetty

As winter 1904 came on we all became very concerned about Evan. He frequently had asthma attacks and with the usual winter bronchitis he was barely able to work on some days.

The crisis came on 7th December when he had a serious asthma attack while he was at work. His fellow jeweller and friend George Nicholls brought him home in a cab. Evan could barely get his breath. George helped get him up the stairs and into bed. Then he went for the doctor and came back to the Jewellery Quarter to where we were living in Hockley Street to tell me Susannah wanted me urgently. I hurried as quickly as my old legs would let me and when I arrived panting, at Wellington Road, Evan's Mam Sarah, his sister Alice and Susannah were gathered round his bed. The atmosphere was sombre and they were all quietly weeping.

"My son, my dear son," Sarah said as she stroked his brow.

Evan's face was grey and he was fighting for every breath. The doctor had been but there was little he could do to help. Susannah sat by him at the head of the bed, a wet handkerchief screwed up in her hand. Evan was propped up on pillows to ease his breathing but nothing was helping him. As the day wore on he lost consciousness and died during the evening. The doctor came at about ten o'clock and confirmed that Evan was dead. "I'm so sorry Mrs Voyce," he said to Susannah, "Far too young to die and leave you."

She was inconsolable, her beloved husband had died at the young age of forty-three and they had only been married for fourteen years. She could not comprehend that he had passed away and lay on her bed stroking his inert hand and weeping. Alice, no stranger to sadness herself, had put Hetty to bed earlier in the evening and had broken the sad news to the other three children. She and I comforted them as best we could. Sidney tried to put on a brave face but Florry and Walter clung to Alice and we all wept together.

Later the undertakers came and Evan's body was laid out and his coffin was placed in the front room as is the custom. The curtains there would remain closed until after the funeral and during that time Susannah went in there for part of every day and family members and close friends came to view the body and to pay their respects.

Sarah was bereft; her eldest son was dead. He had been the baby she was already carrying when she and Charley were married at St Martin's in the Bullring in October 1860. She went back through the years of his life; his birth and babyhood in the tiny cottage in Castle Bromwich; his first steps as she rejoiced in having a son; the way he had played with the other children and been an elder brother to Thomas and to his sisters and finally a much older brother to Harry; how he had become a jeweller and made beautiful jewellery. How could it be that her son had died before herself and Charley? How could it be that he was gone? Charley sat next to her on the sofa in the front room in Susannah's house patting her hand as he stared straight ahead into space. Around ten o'clock he put his arm round her and took her home. They were as united in their grief as they had been in the happy occasions in their lives.

While Sarah turned up the lamp Charley went over to the shelves beside the range and took down the Family Bible and put it on the table. "Charley, what are you doing?" He opened the book at the first page and pointed to the writing there,

"Look here, Sarah, at all these births and deaths recorded in this Bible since the year 1800 when my father John was born. Here is his sister Elizabeth born in 1808. And then my brother Thomas who only lived for three years; my brother John born in 1833; my sister Elizabeth in 1835; then me and finally Mary in 1838; she died the following year." He fetched the bottle of ink and removed the cork from it. He pulled out a chair and sat down at the table. Sarah looked over his shoulder.

"Who was Thomas Voice who died in 1841?"

"He was my grandfather, son of Alexander and Elizabeth and the story goes that he and his brother Hugh came down the Chester Road from Flint in North Wales where they were born. Alexander settled in Castle Bromwich and Hugh settled in Coleshill. I remember writing in all the birth dates of our children and I thought they would be writing our deaths in here next."

"And now you are making the entry for our eldest son."

"Yes, me duck, I am indeed and doing it with a very heavy heart."

Sarah watched as Charley dipped the pen in the ink and laboriously wrote next to Evan's date of birth entry. 'Died 7th December 1904'. She handed him the blotting paper and watched as the heavy book was put back on the shelf. He turned back to Sarah, looked down at her eyes full of tears and then for the first time ever he wept; they wept together with their arms around each other.

I slept on the sofa at Susannah's that night and kept the fire going as it was so cold. In the morning when Hetty started to cry I went to dress her and brought her down stairs for her breakfast. I thought she was oblivious to the family drama that had taken place when she toddled around chatting in her own baby language but then she started to say, "Dada, Dada," so maybe she had missed her Pa as he was always there in the morning. When they heard Hetty downstairs the other children crept down too. Sidney was very quiet and stood gazing out of the window but Florry and Walter came to me and I wrapped my arms round them. "Has my pa really gone for ever?" Walter asked me, his bottom lip quivering.

"Yes my love, he's gone to be with the angels."

"I don't want him to be with the angels. I want him here with us." Florry cried.

"We all do, my dear."

I spread some dripping on bread for their breakfast and made a pot of tea. When they had finished Sidney put on his thick coat and went outside. On this early December day it was just beginning to get light. Outside in the street people were going to work as usual and the milk cart was rattling over the cobblestones. The horse with his mouth in his nosebag was munching at his oats while the milkman put milk in the churns and jugs people had left on their doorsteps. Out there it was a normal day but inside this house was a place of sadness where life, as it had been known, was changed for ever.

Susannah came down soon afterwards and seeing Walter and Florry standing by the table went to them and folded them in her arms. "My darlings," she murmured to them and for several moments they all clung together. Then she turned to me and I could see from the shadows under her eyes that she had not slept that night. "Good morning Ma, not that any morning now can be a good morning."

"I've got a pot of tea brewing my dear. Are you going to

have a cup?"

"Yes, that would be good but I can't eat a thing just now. Where's Sidney?"

I looked through the kitchen window and I could see Sidney and his grandpa in the garden.

"He's out there with his grandpa. They're a comfort to each other."

"Ma, I've been thinking someone has to go and register the death. Would you go for me?"

"Yes, of course I will. I'll go on my way home."

"Yesterday I was a wife, today I am a widow. Everything can change in a few hours. Oh Ma, I don't know how I can bear this," she said gazing into the fire as the tears trickled down her face.

"Susannah, think of the children and be brave."

"Yes, you are right of course and I would be very grateful if you could go and register my poor Evan's death."

So off I went with a heavy heart. The registrar, Mr Price, wrote down all the details as I gave the answers to his questions.

"Where and when did the death occur?"

"The seventh of December at Rock Cottages, Wellington Road."

"Name of deceased?"

"Charles Evan Voyce."

"Age?"

"Forty-three."

"Occupation?"

"Jeweller journeyman."

"Cause of death?"

"Bronchitis, Asthma." I handed him the certificate that Doctor Morris had issued.

"And your name Madam?"

"I am Mary Hall, mother in law of the deceased."

Mr Price completed the certificate by adding the date, the eighth of December, and signing the document.

He stood up and shook my hand.

"Please Madam, give my condolences to the family especially to your daughter Mrs Voyce, the widow."

As I left his office and turned towards home I realised that, yes, my poor Susannah was now a widow. The second widow in our family in the last three years, first Clara and now Susannah. Her sister in law Alice had also been recently widowed. We would never know if Nimrod had left a widow on some foreign shore. As I went along the grey December streets I thought to myself there had been too many deaths, too many by far.

Nearly a year ago the family had gathered for happy Christmas celebrations but now they came from afar for the funeral on Dec 12th at St Mary's. Tilly and Richard came from Yorkshire and Harry came up from Kent with Lizzie and Henry. Thomas and a heavily pregnant Annie came from close by and Alice and Winifred came with Charley and Sarah. All the ladies were in deep mourning black; the men wore black ties and dark coats to keep out the winter chill. When William said he would come with me I was quite surprised but pleased that he wanted to support his wife and daughter. He had respected Evan, realising I suppose what a fine young man he had been and what a terrible loss his death was to Susannah.

I was proud of young Sidney as he escorted his mother and sister into the church. At not far off fourteen years of age he was already trying hard to assume the mantle of man of the house and to be supportive to his mother. Our dear Evan was laid to rest in the churchyard. Susannah had recovered her composure, at least when she was with other people and had told Sidney and Florry that she expected them all to be dignified and if they wanted to cry they were to do it in private. It was a lot to ask of a ten year old girl but Florry managed well until it was time to throw a handful of earth into the grave on top of her father's coffin. "Grandma, I can't do that," she whispered to me."

"That's all right Florry, you don't have to."

On that dreary December day the group of mourners around the grave consisted of friends as well as members of the family. George Nicholls who had brought Evan home when he collapsed in his workshop was there with

Elizabeth, his wife. He had been most kind to Susannah. Walter and Hetty were too young to attend their father's funeral but after it was all over they took flowers to his grave. It was a sad day and I have become increasingly weary of life. There has been too much sadness both in our family and for those around us. Now my legs trouble me and I get out of breath easily. I am old and I am tired of life.

But in his old age William has mellowed. I think he is sorry for the trouble he has caused all through the years and he tries to make up for it now by being more thoughtful and showing some kindness to me. Of an evening he'll sometimes fetch a bottle of beer from the 'Off Licence' and we'll sit and reminisce about the times we've been through. We leave out the bad bits and remember the good times of which there were some.

Susannah had been through many trials and tribulations in the last years and her struggle went on stoically. Eventually her life regained its purpose which was to live for her children and especially for Walter.

Chapter Eight

Widowhood 1904-1914

Susannah continues -

I could not sleep at night after Evan died but, on those dark days before Christmas it was so cold downstairs before the fire was lit that it was warmer to stay alone in the bed that for fourteen years had held the two of us. I used to reach out to where my beloved had slept and there was a cold and empty space. The stone hot water bottle I had taken to bed with me was no longer even slightly warm. I was bereft. I realised that never more would his arms enfold me; never more would we be able to comfort each other. In the dark hours of the night as I shed my tears I had never felt more alone.

But the funeral was over and Walter and Florry were sent back to school. I had put black armbands on their coats as is the custom so everyone would know what had happened. We just had to struggle on and make the best of things. It was hard, so very hard. Each morning I put a match to a candle and went downstairs in the dark to the back kitchen and lit the fire. It was a little more cheerful when the flames crackled under the kindling; sometimes there was a glowing ember or two and the fire was still alight from the night before if I had banked it up well with wet slack. Then by using the bellows I would soon have a blaze going so that I could heat a kettle of water and rub my hands together to warm them up.

That first morning after the funeral when I had stirred the fire into action and before the children were up I pulled my shawl round my shoulders, opened the door quietly and went into the cold, dark front room where Evan's coffin had been for the last week. I had been in there every day but now even his body was gone. I looked round the room with new eyes; at the piano which he had played and where as a family we had gathered round and sung; at his rack of pipes; at the family photos on the table by the window and at his armchair where on a Sunday afternoon after dinner he would read the paper in front of the fire while I washed up, usually with Florry's help.

Oh, how I was going to miss him in so many ways. And as I stood there in the cold and gloom I remembered that just under a year ago we had all been together as a family at Christmas in this room. It had been such a happy time. What a good thing we cannot see into the future because it would spoil our enjoyment of the present. I stifled a sob as I heard the door open behind me. Sidney, unheard, had crept down the stairs and come to find me. Dear boy, he put his arms round me and said, "Ma, I'm the man of the house now. I will look after you. Don't fret."

"Sidney, my dear, thank you for those kind words. They mean the world to me." And I held him close.

And in the following years Sidney kept to his word. Each week as he came through the door on pay day he handed his pay packet over to me and it was much needed as it was almost the only money we had coming in until Florry went into service three years later. We decided to buy some more laying hens so there would be a surplus of eggs to sell and Sidney doubled his efforts in the garden to grow all the vegetables we needed. We even contemplated fattening a pig on any kitchen scraps we had, but eventually I felt that was a step too far.

I took in sewing, mainly from the ladies in the big houses in Handsworth Wood who wanted dresses made and so we got by, just. It was now that I was particularly pleased that I had my Singer sewing machine. Alice had found it for me soon after we were married when she came across a second hand treadle machine for sale, no longer needed by someone who was giving up dressmaking. Sidney often complained about all the half-made clothes that were hanging around so in the end I reorganised the bedrooms upstairs so that Sidney and Walter continued to share a room and Florry had Hetty in with her. I stayed in the larger bedroom that Evan and I had used but turned it into my sewing room as well. I had found a smaller bed and so it worked out well. Nevertheless when I sold the big bed that I had shared with my dearest one, where all the children had been born and where he had died I suffered a few pangs of remorse.

I made all our clothes as well. But there was no money for extras, it all had to go on food that we couldn't grow and shoes and the other absolute necessities of life like the rent and coal. I knew that if we ever got so low as to have to apply for Parish Relief we'd have to sell the piano first and I certainly didn't want that to happen.

Sarah came in most days from next door. She was missing her tall, handsome son dreadfully but we both knew it was no good crying over spilt milk. We gave each other a hug and just had to get on with life and not make a fuss. She and Charley were amazing they just squared their shoulders and carried on. But Charley's eyes didn't twinkle like they used to, not for a long time. Christmas that first year was just impossible coming less than a month after dear Evan had left us. Florry voiced everyone's feelings when her eyes filled with tears and she twirled a lock of her dark hair round a finger and said, "It just isn't Christmas without our Pa." But as usual we soldiered on and there was always Hetty to cheer us up. She was too young to understand what had happened and everyone played with her and made her laugh. The sound of laughter is a great tonic.

Thomas and Annie, as always, were good friends to me. Thomas had been very grieved to lose his elder brother and now took over the role of elder son in his parents' lives. Annie's next baby, Henry Joseph, was born two days after Christmas. The coming of a new life so soon after one had been lost reminded us all that the pattern of life continues. Annie was busier than ever as she now had six sons and one daughter. It was good to see their happy family. The year had turned and it was now 1905. As the long, dark days of winter gave way to the lighter days of February and March our spirits began to lift a little.

When I was pegging out the washing one sunny Monday morning I gazed around at the new growth. Snowdrops clustered under the apple trees and yellow and purple crocuses were as bright as jewels in the borders, Florry's new tabby kitten ran and jumped as she chased a dried up leaf down the pathway and a blackbird with a bright yellow beak tugged away at an unlucky worm in Sidney's carrot patch. The sun was warm on my back and helped to ease my taut muscles. I thought to myself, maybe my life hadn't totally ended. There was beauty all around me and I had my dear children. Their future would be my life. I would live through them.

Florry was now almost eleven and was a great help to me both in the house and in looking after Hetty who was now into her second year and chattering away and getting into everything. In another year or so I would have to face losing Florry as she would undoubtedly go out into the world to find work as a live-in maid. Sidney had just had his fourteenth birthday and had been working for a year. He seemed to enjoy being a gardener and working in the fresh air. But my main hopes for the future had begun to rest on Walter. His school reports made me glow with pride. They were full of praise for him in every subject.

A few weeks before the school broke up for the summer holidays I had a letter from Walter's headmaster asking me to go and see him. I smartened myself up and made a bit of an effort with my clothes. Pushing open the school gate, going across the school yard and into the corridor leading to the Headmaster's office reminded me of that dreadful day when I had been summoned to see another headmaster, Mr Davenport on the day that I had been dismissed from my job as a pupil teacher. Well that couldn't be the reason this time. But had Walter committed a dreadful crime I wondered?

When I tapped nervously at the door a booming voice cried, "Come in!"

So I opened the door and in I went to a rather dark, book

lined room with a large teachers' desk, on which were piles of exercise books. In front of me a tall scholarly looking man with a receding hairline had risen to his feet and was holding his hand out to shake mine. "Ah, good afternoon Mrs Voyce. What a pleasure it is to see you. Come and sit down."

"Good afternoon sir," Obviously no one was in trouble, so what could this summons mean?

"I expect you are wondering why I have asked to you to come and see me. Well the thing is that your young Walter is showing great promise and I want him to take the Grammar School entrance exam next year. I think he has a very good chance indeed of passing it. Now that would please you wouldn't it, to have a son at Handsworth Grammar School?"

"It certainly would sir but I am a widow and my financial circumstances are very straitened. I simply could not afford to pay for him to go there even if he did pass the entrance exam."

"There may be a way round that because I think he is so gifted that he will quite probably get a Scholarship, which would mean that you wouldn't have to pay the school fees. Now what do you say to that?"

"This is such a surprise that I don't quite know what to think."

"Come now, Mrs Voyce, how can you possibly have any doubts? A son at the Grammar School taking up a free place? Goodness knows where it might lead, to university perhaps."

Well, what could I do but agree to Walter being entered for the examination?

As I walked back home up Wellington Road my mind was in a turmoil; Walter at Grammar School; Walter possibly going to university in the years to come. Birmingham University had received its Royal Charter in 1900. Is that where he might go in the future? New exciting possibilities were opening up and for the first time since my darling Evan's death I began to feel quite uplifted. I had realised some time ago that my future happiness rested with the future of my children; now the future was beginning to materialise in undreamed of ways. I was going to be so proud of Walter. The only sadness was that Evan wasn't here to share in all of this.

Well no, that wasn't true. It wasn't the only sadness. Unfortunately there were other family members who had sad events in their lives as well. This time it was a tragedy that struck Thomas and Annie and their family on Saturday 1st July. The weather had been wonderful that week and when a heavily pregnant Annie sent Len off to get some coal on the Saturday afternoon no-one could have foreseen that the errand would end in tragedy. He found his friend Tom and they went together. When they passed the canal near Spring Hill Len said, "It's so hot. Let's go for a dip."

Len made sure his ball, his tin for catching interesting objects and his Saturday penny were safely stowed away in his trouser pockets and the two boys took off their clothes down to their underpants and plunged into the cool water.

They had a great time splashing each other, climbing out onto the bank and then jumping in again. After a while Tom climbed out and looked round for Len. "Len, where are you?" He looked up and down nearby but nowhere could he see his friend. With mounting panic he called again, "Len, stop mucking around. Where are you hiding?"

But Len wasn't mucking around. He had sunk beneath the water. By now a small crowd was gathering alerted by Tom's cries. Tom bravely dived into the water again and again until he had located Len and then he brought him to the surface. Eager hands reached down to help pull him out. Tom climbed out and someone said, "You got to do artificial respiration on him." Tom wasn't too sure exactly how to do this but he moved Len's arms backwards and forwards until some men came up and took over with the correct technique. Sadly it was to no avail. On that beautiful sunny afternoon poor little Len aged nine, had lost his life.

In the evening Thomas came round to Wellington Road and told us the sad news. "Annie says can you go round?" He said. So I left what I was doing and hurried round immediately. The curtains had been drawn in the front parlour, the undertakers had been and there was poor Len in his coffin and a very tearful Annie gazing at her son and sobbing. "Susannah, he was full of himself only a few hours ago and now look what's happened. I told him to stay away from the canal. There's all sorts of things under the water to get caught up on."

"Boys will be boys," I said, "but not usually with such disastrous results. Come on my love, we'll put the kettle on and sit in the back kitchen till Thomas comes back."

So that's what we did and talked about the children and the problems they caused.

A few days later the funeral was held. A child's funeral is always very upsetting and for me additionally it was only six months or so since my beloved Evan had been buried. Life is sometimes unbearably hard. The rest of Thomas and Annie's children were thriving and barely six weeks after poor Len had lost his life, Annie's son Sidney Howard was born on the 16th August. No child can replace another one but at least by caring for baby Sidney her mind was occupied with new life.

In September her eldest son Charles Thomas, now fifteen came home one day with the good news that he'd found himself a job as a lorry boy on the railway at Hockley. His work involved loading up the steam driven lorries and his wage of nine shillings a week went straight to Annie who was glad that he had started contributing to the family finances. She gave him back a shilling of his wages on the understanding that he would now buy his own clothes.

So with the prospect of the Grammar School Entrance examination in the next few months I spent some time with Walter every day going through his school work with him. Fortunately my years as a teacher had given me a very good idea of the subjects that we should be concentrating on. He was of course already a very proficient reader and so we made sure that when he had to write an essay the spelling and grammar would be perfect. We read newspapers and studied atlases; we read history books and made sure we knew as much as possible about the British

Empire.

We didn't neglect Mathematics either and polished up long division and long multiplication; multiplication tables of course had been mastered some years earlier. We did endless mental arithmetic sums and calculated how long it would take a bath to overflow if the tap was pouring water into it at such and such a rate. Calculations involving pounds, shillings, pennies and farthings were common place as were those with miles, chains, furlongs, yards, feet and inches not to mention gallons, quarts, pints and gills. We became thoroughly conversant with averages and fractions plus some geometry and algebra. Walter thrived on all of this. To Florry and Sidney it was as if we were talking a foreign language.

And the day of the exam finally arrived. I gave Walter a hug as he got ready to leave the house.

"Just do your best my dear," I said encouragingly.

"I will Ma, I'll make you proud of me yet."

"I already am Walter."

I was anxious to hear how he had got on when he came home at the end of the afternoon. "I think I answered most of the questions, so probably all right." he said." But there were some boys there who didn't seem to have a clue as to the right way to go about it. They larked around and at dinner time went off to the games shed and got out the cricket equipment to play with so when they went back in for the afternoon session they were all hot and bothered. Didn't seem the right sort for Grammar School at all."

"Now don't start getting high and mighty," I admonished him." Maybe it's just that they didn't have a mother to help them in the way you have."

24. Possibly Walter, Sidney and Charley, Wellington Road c1907

He gave me a cheeky grin and went off to kick a football around at the front of the house. We had to wait for several weeks until the results came. And then one morning when we were sitting at the table just finishing our breakfast the post arrived and there was a crisp white envelope with the Grammar School crest on it. Walter and I looked at each other and my heart started to beat faster. He stood by me as I nervously slid a paper knife along the top of the envelope and gently eased out the folded paper it contained. I opened the letter and started to read it. A smile spread across my face, "Walter you've done it," I said, "you've won the scholarship. In September you will be going to Handsworth Grammar School." Behind us, still at the table, Sidney mimicked his Welsh grandmother and said,

"There's posh we are!"

Florry got up and flung her arms round Walter,

"Well done little brother. It's nice to know someone in the family has brains."

Three year old Hetty, sensing the excitement of the morning sat on the floor banging a wooden spoon against an old saucepan lid I had given her to play with. I suddenly glanced at the clock on the mantelpiece. "Children," I cried, "look at the time! Florry and Walter, you'll be late for school and Sidney you've got to go to work." And so we came back to earth with a bump and endeavoured to resume our normal lives. When I went next door and told Sarah and Charley of Walter's success they were delighted.

"The first person in our family to go to Grammar School," Charley purred.

"There's posh we are," Sarah said and then wondered why I seemed amused.

"I was just thinking the same thing myself Mam."

From time to time Harry would come up from London and bring us up to date with his news. When he came to see us one week-end that summer he was full of life as always. With twinkly eyes, just like Charley, he bragged to the children, "Well me ducks, the latest is that I am a policeman. The Army, no less, said what a good chap I am so I've got a job working for the London, Brighton and South Coast Railway Company."

Sidney said, "I didn't know they had policemen on the railway. What do you have to do?"

"Ah laddie I deal with TROUBLE makers," he said in a growly voice to frighten them. "So you watch your P's and Q's when you're on the train or your Uncle Harry will hear all about it and come and clap a pair of handcuffs on you."

I had to laugh at Harry. He was irrepressible.

"Actually I mainly work at the goods depot at Willow Walk. Theft is the thing to watch and then sometimes I'm at Newhaven watching for people smuggling goods in from France."

As the summer drew to a close the question of Walter's uniform for his new school arose. There was no problem in making his grey trousers. For the first year or two he would still be in short trousers with white shirts which I could make but I could not make the blazer that he would have to wear. Sarah and Charley said they would buy that as a reward for his successful examination result. I was very relieved as those blazers are expensive and then there's the badge that has to be sewn on. Very smart it is too. I bought his school tie and cap.

In September he commenced the first of his seven years at the Grammar School where he was very successful. He worked hard, was popular and as time went on became a member of the school football team. He'd told me that he would make me proud of him and I was, very proud indeed.

The following summer, soon after the post arrived one morning, Sarah came bustling round with a letter she had just received. "Look at this Susannah," she said with a great beaming smile, "news from Harry. He's found himself a young lady and wants to bring her here for our approval. She's called Eleanor"

"Oh that's wonderful news Mam."

"Yes, isn't it? Just think, my wayward youngest son may be about to settle down at last."

"So when are they coming?"

"Next week end I think. I was wondering if Eleanor could sleep in Florry's bed as Florry is in service now."

"Of course she can. I'll get it ready for her tomorrow. She'll have to put up with sharing with Hetty though."

Oh I'm sure she'll not find your Hetty a problem. I gather she's got several brothers and sisters so she'll be used to the hurley burley of family life."

Florry had recently left home and was now a live-in servant just as I had once been. She wasn't far away and we loved to see her back at home whenever she had a few hours off duty. So her bed was made ready for Eleanor and Hetty promised to keep her room tidy and to be especially kind to Eleanor.

So we were all agog the following week end to see Harry's young lady. I must say he had very good taste for she was charming. Knowing how cocky Harry could be we were somewhat amused by the transformation in him. I think he was really quite self-conscious. And in a quiet moment when she was with his parents he slipped round to see me next door. "Well Susannah what do you think? Isn't she a smasher?"

"Indeed she is Harry. I'm so happy for you."

So it was no surprise to hear that Harry and Eleanor had become engaged a few weeks later. The 4th of January was the date that had been set for the wedding. They were married in Eleanor's home parish of Bromley, at St Michael's Church. When Charley and Sarah went down for the wedding on the train Alice went as well to see her little brother married and to make sure that Charley and Sarah were all right on the journey. St Michael's was not far from where Lizzie and Henry were living at Bexley, so although Thomas and Annie didn't manage to get to the wedding and neither did I there were several members of the family there.

In the Autumn Hetty started school. As she and I had had plenty of time together I had been able to teach her to read before she went to school and she took to it like a duck to water and proved like Walter to be an able pupil.

In 1910 as the family gathered once more for Christmas in Wellington Road there was concern at how frail Charley had become. But there was also much to be thankful for. Harold had married Eleanor the previous year. Walter was doing well at the Grammar School and Sidney was established as a gardener. Lizzie came up from Kent with her husband Henry and Harold and Esther came north with them on the train from London. Tilly and her husband Richard had stayed in Yorkshire with their four children. On Christmas Eve Harry, Henry and Sidney went off to the Bull Ring Market to find a Christmas tree for Charley and Sarah's home and also one for ours.

There was a flurry of cooking to be done while the men were out at the market. Puddings had been made weeks beforehand and were maturing in the larder. I had made a Christmas cake iced with marzipan and white icing and Sidney had killed two of his largest chickens. So we all put aprons on and Sarah and Eleanor stuffed the chickens with sausage meat at one end and a delicious sage and onion stuffing at the other while Florry helped me to make a stack of mince pies. The family she worked for had gone away to relations in the south for Christmas so she was able to be with us. Six year old Hetty put her apron on and stood on a chair at the kitchen table and helped to fill the pies with spicy mincemeat that I had made a few weeks earlier.

When the men came home with the trees Florry and Hetty decorated the one in our parlour and Alice and Winifred decorated the one that stood in Sarah and Charley's home. Walter and Sidney placed sprigs of holly around both homes and put up some paper streamers that Hetty and I had made. It all looked very festive.

On Christmas morning Henry, Lizzie, Harry and Eleanor walked to church with the children while Alice and I continued with the preparations for the family Christmas dinner. Charley and Sarah sat quietly by the fire gathering up their strength for the day ahead.

After a while I slipped away and went into our parlour and spent a few moments thinking of my dear Evan and our last Christmas together seven years ago. It was now just over six years since he had died. My heart still grieved for him. Life had been hard but with the support of Sarah and Charley we had survived, the children were thriving and I realised I had a lot to be thankful for. Over the years there had been so many deaths and my parents, Mary and William, had also passed away during those last six years.

We had a splendid Christmas Dinner. It was good to see so many of the family members together. Harry and Henry took the children out for a brisk walk in the park afterwards. We put Charley in his favourite chair by the fire so he could have a nap and the rest of us did the washing up and started to prepare a stack of sandwiches for tea. Thomas and Annie were coming round with their seven children. The house would be bursting at the seams.

After tea Walter, Sidney and Winifred organised parlour games and charades. It was all great fun and very noisy. Eventually Thomas and Annie took their brood home and a relative peace returned after all the excitement of the day. Later, Charley and Sarah came into our parlour and Sarah requested that we should sing some carols round the fire. Alice and I took it in turns to play the piano. Hetty sang 'Away in a Manger' for us. I wished my dear Evan could have seen her with the firelight reflected on her pretty blond curls. It had been a tiring day and during the singing of 'Silent Night' I turned to look at Charley. He was fast asleep.

Only five days later he died quietly in his sleep. The death certificate simply records 'heart disease'. What a dear man he had been, such a comfort and support to me in my years of widowhood. But for Sarah it was devastating. They had been together for fifty years. She would be lost without him. With concern for her father mounting Lizzie had stayed on after Christmas and after he had died it was she who went to register his death.

At the funeral, Sarah, dressed in black, looked a sad, lonely, little old lady. But it was easy to see what a matriarch she was of the Voice family when they were all lined up behind her going into the church for the service. Thomas, as her eldest surviving son, escorted her followed by Annie, then Tilly with Richard and their family down from Yorkshire, Lizzie had stayed on to comfort Sarah after Charley died and Henry had come up from Kent again with Harry and Eleanor. Alice and Winifred were next and I followed with Sidney, Florry and Walter. It had been decided that any of the grandchildren who were twelve or older would be allowed to attend the funeral so that meant that of my children Sidney, Florry and Walter were there. Charley's seventy seven year old brother John decided to come in on the train from Castle Bromwich with his wife Susanna. It was a sad day as Charley had been dearly loved by a wide circle of people.

Increasingly over the years as Charley grew older Sidney had taken on more and more of the garden belonging to the two houses. Now of course it was his to do with as he wished but he made few changes and we continued to have fresh eggs, fresh vegetables and flowers for the two houses.

My continuing joy was Walter who was a star pupil at the Grammar School. In his school reports his teachers kept mentioning that he was university material and as we moved into 1914 the possibility of him staying on at school for another year was spoken of and trying for the Oxford Scholarship. I felt so proud of my son. What a glowing future beckoned him. How proud my dear Evan would have been to have a son who was an undergraduate at Oxford.

Chapter Nine

The Great War and Beyond 1914-1924

Sarah concludes the family story:

It all happened so long ago and I am so very old now; eighty-eight. After all the terrible events of the Great War my memory sometimes plays tricks on me. Did Walter actually go to Oxford before he joined up or was it hoped that he would go or is the whole idea just a figment of my imagination? I know it was Susannah's dearest wish that he should go but now she too is gone so I cannot ask her. But I know I must make a great effort to think clearly and really remember what happened.

Susannah had great hopes for her younger son. Indeed after Evan's untimely death in 1904 she pinned all her hopes, all her future, on Walter. But the assassination of Archduke Franz Ferdinand in Sarajevo in July 1914 changed our lives forever as it did for millions of other people.

The summer of 1914 was when the nightmare started but at first it all seemed so far away. We didn't see how it could possibly affect us. The wrangling went on between Germany, France, Russia, Serbia and Austro-Hungary and war was getting closer and closer. Finally as Germany declined to reply to the British ultimatum about Belgium the die was cast.

When Harry came home from the Boer War he'd always said that if ever there was another war he would join up again immediately. At the end of July he and Eleanor came up from London for an unexpected but welcome visit. This time he was not the irrepressible Harry of his youth. The fighting in Africa and his work as a Railway Policeman had made him more serious but he was still, at thirty-two years of age, my much loved youngest son, albeit that Charley and I had adopted him. When they arrived he gave me a big hug and we chatted over a cup of tea. "Mam, you've got to know that as a reservist I've been told not to be out of touch. I'm afraid war is coming and as soon as it does I shall have to go."

"Oh Harry I wish it didn't have to be this way." And turning to Eleanor I said, "And what do you think about all this my dear?"

"I don't want him to go," she said wistfully, "but he's always made it clear to me that he's a soldier at heart, so it has to be that way."

That evening we had a family gathering with Susannah and her family and Thomas and Annie came round with some of their children. It was almost like old times with so many of the family together. How they were all growing up and where had the years gone to? And still there were spaces in our hearts for my Charley who had died only four years ago and Evan who had been gone for ten years. Harry looked over at Charles Thomas and Walter. "So will you two join up if war comes?" He asked them.

Susannah quickly butted in, "Walter may have another year at school Harry and then university perhaps so hopefully it will all be over before then."

"Well we all hope it will be over soon. And what about you Charley?" He said turning to Thomas's oldest son.

"Oh he's courting Harry. He doesn't want to think about war," said Annie.

Thomas looked on, "Well there you are Harry. It seems the mothers of these two youngsters are going to keep them here by hook or by crook."

"Do mothers ever want their sons to go to war?" I said.

"They might if they came back covered in glory having fought for their country," he replied.

"As long as they do come back," Eleanor added sombrely.

To try to lighten the atmosphere I looked at Charles Thomas and said,

"Now young man, what's all this about you courting?"

"Her name is Charlotte, Grandma and I'm going to marry her one day."

"Well in that case bring her to see me and I'll tell you if she's good enough for you."

Harry and Eleanor left for home the next day. Harry had come to me earlier in the day and said,

"Mam in case I never come back I want you to know what a special mother you have been to me. I have never felt other than your true son."

Of course that brought tears to my eyes, no words would come. I just held him close to me. It was with a heavy heart that the farewell hugs were made and as I waved to them when they went off down Wellington Road I wondered if I would ever see my dear boy again.

A few days later, as all the world now knows, Germany declined to reply to the telegram demanding that the Kaiser remove his troops from Belgium. It was now nearly midnight on August 4th 1914 and we were at war with Germany. And on that day Harry was recalled to active service in the Coldstream Guards departing soon afterwards for France and leaving Eleanor alone in London.

Everywhere there was a huge surge of patriotism. The poster of Lord Kitchener, of whom we had heard so much during the Boer War, was everywhere. 'Your country needs you!' It said with a picture of Lord Kitchener pointing straight out at you. It was mesmerizing. The queues of young men keen to go to fight for King and country lined the streets, with some youngsters saying they were older than they really were so they could enlist. Many of them thought it would be a great lark, a wonderful adventure and often they joined up with their friends and so groups of them from the same street, the same football club, the same workplace joined up and went off together with people they knew. They were called 'The Pals Brigades'. Everybody said they'd all be home again by Christmas anyway.

Poor, deluded souls. Little did they know of the horrors that lay ahead of them in the trenches; little did they know that many of them would not come home again; that there were towns and streets where every other house had lost a son, a father, a husband or a lover. Sometimes in a family two or more sons would be taken. It was tragedy on a large scale. Some of the postmen resigned because they couldn't stand the anguish caused by the numerous letters they had to deliver announcing a death.

This time I had no Charley to support me when our youngest son went off to war although for as long as she was able to dear Susannah next door was everything one could wish for in a daughter in law. Thomas and Annie were not far away, neither was Alice. Her daughter Winifred continued to live with me for several years and it was good to have someone else in the house. Florry's job as a live in housemaid was only about a mile away on Birchfield Road and of course Susannah, Sidney, Walter and Hetty were still next door.

At the end of August Alderman W. H. Bowater, Deputy Mayor of the City of Birmingham, made an appeal for a non-manual Battalion. In one week four thousand five hundred recruits had come forward forming three strong Battalions. Already eight thousand men had enlisted through the usual channels.

Susannah had very mixed feelings when Walter became one of these young men. Her hopes and dreams of him going to university had to be postponed but she was proud of her son for doing his duty as Harry had known she would be. Walter was in the 15th Battalion Royal Warwickshire Regiment (2nd Birmingham Battalion).The first parade was in the grounds of the General Hospital and then there was a march to Edgbaston Park where it seems some basic marching technique may have been acquired. After that everyone went home again to await their call up notices. On the 11th October the battalion had a service at St Martin's Church in the Bull Ring. Later I reminded Walter that that was where Charley and I had been married fifty-four years earlier in 1860. After that came a lengthy training period in Sutton Park not so very far away from Wellington Road, so when he was off duty we were still able to see quite a lot of Walter which was a comfort to his mother.

Charles Thomas brought his young lady, Charlotte, to see me in due course. She was a pretty girl and sensible. He had chosen well and they made a charming couple. In October he came to me and said, "Grandma, Charlotte and I are getting married next week and then I'm going to join up. I have to serve my country. I'm joining the Rifle Brigade."

"I admire your patriotism," I told him but inwardly my heart was heavy at the news that a third member of our family was going off to the war. They were married on 18thOctober when he was twenty-four. Their son Charles William was born the following May.

Thomas and Annie joined us on the following Sunday evening as usual and Susannah was there as well. "So your Charley has gone off to war then Annie?" Susannah said. Annie sniffed and dabbed her eyes,

"Yes, I'm afraid he has but sad as I am to see him go I'm also proud that he's gone off to serve his country."

"That's just how I feel Annie," said Susannah placing a comforting hand on Annie's shoulder, "but it's been a wrench for me to give up the hope that he would go to university."

"Maybe that will come after the war."

With three members of the family now enlisted in the army I felt Sidney was getting side-lined here but there was no question if him going to war because he had a weak chest. Increasingly it was looking as if he had inherited that problem from his father and of course the army had turned him down on medical grounds. In fact, looking back at Sidney's life he'd been cast into the background on numerous occasions. When he was very small Evan and Susannah had had the distressing problem of baby Ethel to deal with just at the time when he needed encouragement. Later, after Evan had died, Susannah very noticeably favoured Walter as her bright hope for the future and now poor Sidney couldn't serve his country because he was medically unfit to do so. He still had his gardening though and he was very successful with that. In some ways he was even more in demand now that so many able bodied men had gone off to war.

"Grandma," he'd say to me with a wry smile, "there's just me and the men too old to fight doing it now. Sometimes people look at me as if to say, 'Why are you still here young man?' Someone even pushed a white feather at me, but I'm not a coward, I'm just not fit enough to go. Still I don't say anything. I just go and vent my anger on some digging."

Poor Sidney I thought, there's a lot going on in that mind

that we don't know about. And what of Susannah's two girls? Well Florry was still a live-in housemaid on Birchfield Road and Hetty was a school girl, so no problems there.

Another figure appearing more and more in Susannah's life was George Nicholls who had been a friend of Evan. His wife had died a year or so back and I think he and Susannah enjoyed each other's company. There was no reason for either of them to be lonely just because they had both lost their life partners. And me? Yes of course I missed my beloved Charley. But time heals and I sat by the fire and lived again through my memories. I would never forget his love, his twinkly eyes and his steadfastness.

The letter when it came was quite unexpected. Harry was a survivor, or so I thought. But my dear boy was killed on 21st December 1914. A life sacrificed for his country; a second son of mine dead. Why had this family had so many deaths around the Christmas season? My eldest son, Evan, at the beginning of December ten years ago; my Charley just after Christmas four years ago, and now Harry just before Christmas.

Dear Mrs Voyce,

It is my painful duty to be the bearer of very sad news for you. Your son 2766 Private H.E.Voyce was killed this morning while on duty. He was struck on the head by a piece of shell and death was instantaneous. I regret to say that at the moment we are unable to recover his body.

Your son's death is very much felt by the platoon and he was much esteemed by the officers as a good and manly soldier of the kind we can ill spare. His death is a blow to his comrades.

The officers and men here one and all express our deepest sympathy with you in your sad loss and we hope that your son having died a soldiers death will in some measure console you in your great grief.

With our greatest sympathy

Yours sincerely

O/C

"Susannah!" I cried out when I opened the letter and read it, "Susannah, something terrible has happened"

Dear girl, she came running round at once and I showed her the letter. "Oh Mam. Not dear Harry. I can't believe this. It's just too terrible."

I wept for all of that day. One by one the others came in too and tears were shed. Thomas, Annie, Winifred, Alice, Sidney, Florry and young Hetty. We had all loved Harry. He'd been such a bright note in our lives. Annie put her arms round me, "Oh Mam, we shall miss him so dreadfully and now I am more fearful than ever for my Charley."

"Yes my dear. It fills you with dread doesn't it?"

We didn't forget poor Eleanor in London who must have had a similar letter and Susannah wrote to her on behalf of all of us in Birmingham. Poor woman, married for five years and now a widow. I read later that as an experienced soldier Harry was much valued in those first weeks of the war. Had he lived he would have been very useful for the new armies of 1915. Just like many others his body was never found. I had a recurring nightmare of my dear son being blown apart in the mud and icy conditions of that December. Too awful to contemplate. He died at the battle of Givenchy; a futile loss of life for English soldiers and many Indians and Ghurkhas too, where no gains were made, only losses. He is remembered on the Le Touret Memorial, near Bethune in the Pas de Calais, Northern France.

The informal Christmas truce of that year was due partly to the need for the bodies of the fallen, if they could be found, to be gathered up and buried. The war hadn't finished by Christmas 1914 as many had confidently predicted. Susannah had been sent the Christmas edition of Walter's school magazine called 'The Bridge'. "There is praise here for former scholars who have joined up," she said, knowing that Walter was included in their number.

And so 1915 had dawned, a new year but much the same as the old one. The fighting continued, the horrors in the trenches carried on. The numbers of dead and injured rose and rose. And again in the summer Susannah showed me the latest edition of 'The Bridge' pointing out that, 'The school has great pride in knowing that over two hundred old boys are now serving their country and one master has left and gained a commission.' "And my Walter is one of them," she said, proudly fingering the locket that hung around her neck containing a photograph of Walter in uniform.

25. Walter Charles Voyce

In the summer of 1915 Susannah and George Nicholls were married. I think the worries of the previous year about whether Walter would join up or pursue the idea of university had taken their toll on her and she admitted to feeling increasingly unwell. Knowing that it would not be long before Walter was fighting in France I knew George would be a comfort to her. By this time Walter had gone with the other recruits to Wensleydale for further training and then to Codford on Salisbury Plain. It was then that Susannah realised Walter was in it for real and that before long he would be in the trenches. In November Walter embarked for France. It was almost a year since Harry had been killed. An icy hand of premonition gripped my heart.

At the end of November Susannah received the first of many letters Walter sent from France.

(Author's note: it is probable that place names would have been obliterated by the censor).

'Dear Mother,' he wrote, *'here we are in France. The Transports went from Southampton to Le Havre with horses, mules and carts but most of us came across the sea from Folkestone to Boulogne on the S.S. Invicta. Had a shocking first night under canvas. The blankets were sopping wet and it was freezing and there was no hot food. Hope things improve.*

Your loving son. Walter

A week or so later,

Dearest Mother,

Marching and more marching from village to village until we get to the front line. Some of the chaps can't manage it and have their packs carried for them and even some of them get a ride. Not me. I'm strong. Last night we heard gunfire for the first time and saw the flashes in the night sky from the trench mortars. I guess we must be getting near to the front line. It's all getting more real now. We're wondering what lies ahead.

Your loving son Walter.

PS Give my love to Grandma, Sidney and the girls.

13th December

Dear All,

Now we're camped out in the grounds of a Chateau at Suzanne after more marching. Only a fortnight to Christmas. Can't help thinking of Christmas at home. We're going into the trenches now to learn what it's all about then we're in it for real as we'll be taking over a section of the front line for a month. Walter

A few days later,

Dearest Mother,

The mud here is unbelievable. We hear the trenches were all right until the wet weather came in November, then the mud slid down the sides and collected in the bottom. Moving around is awful. Some chaps get their boots sucked off and one chap lost his trousers too and had to go round in a sand bag with holes for his legs. Worse for the Hun though as their trenches are lower down the hill than ours.

Your loving son,

Walter.

Christmas Day 1915

Dear Everybody at Home,

What a brilliant day we've had. We're back at the Chateau in Suzanne so we are safe. The parcels from home arrived so thank you for the food and chocolate and cigarettes. Hetty's scarf is just the ticket for keeping me warm as are Florry's gloves. I can see you've all been beavering away. A great surprise at dinner time was when Christmas puddings from the Lord Mayor of Birmingham's Fund were handed round. Real Christmas puds, what a treat. We had a merry time.

Happy Christmas and a Happy New Year,

Walter

January 6th

Dear Mother,

We're back at the front now after our break. We have forty-eight hours on the front line followed by forty-eight hours in the Maricourt defences, then another forty-eight hours at the front and then forty-eight hours rest in Suzanne but we're coming out of here on January 10th for some general training back at Sailly Lorette.

Walter

January 25th

Dear Mother,

Thank you for your letter with all the home news.

We've been doing some more general training and been inspected by General C.T. Kavanagh. It's cold but any way the marching warms you up. We'll be on the move again any day now.

Walter

March 3rd

Dear Mother,

More marching and finally it brought us to Arras, where we'll be relieving a French Division for three months. Trenches much better here as they are dug into the chalk. It's bitterly cold and there has been heavy snow. Arras has been badly damaged by enemy shelling especially the station and road junctions. There is light shelling every day with rifle grenades and trench mortars. There are, of course, casualties. Under the town there are many deep cellars and even the sewers have been cleared out and made habitable. There's room for two divisions to be safely housed underground. Walter

15th March

Dear Mother,

More marching and we're now at Rolincourt, a ruined village half a mile behind the line and about three miles from Arras. The rest billets are at Agnez-Les-Duisans. When we are there we sleep and clean our clothes and equipment. There are hot showers there too, Luxury! We also have training parades and church parades on Sundays and we have football matches. Ah me, memories of when I was in the School Team. Seems a million miles and a million years away. And there is a Divisional Concert Party. So you see life is not all bad by any means.

Your loving son

Walter

25th March

Dear Mother,

I forgot to mention the generous supply of socks sent out from Birmingham by the Ladies Committee. I know you and Grandma and the girls are knitting away there. It's very much appreciated. We haven't had a single case of trench foot. Every night with the rations and the daily tot of rum we get a clean pair of socks and before we put them on we have to rub our feet with whale oil, horrid smelly stuff but it's doing the trick and we've all got good feet as a result. So pass the word on and keep knitting.

Love from Walter

April.

Dear Mother,

We had a very important visitor here the other day. No less than the Commander-in-Chief, Sir Douglas Haig, who passed through the village in the afternoon. We mounted a guard of honour for him.

Soon after that there was more marching, back to Arras, this time to relieve the 1ˢᵗ Devons.

The most dangerous thing here at the moment is being part of a group who go out at night to examine the wire. Some of the chaps have metal helmets to protect them but one of the men felt his rear was more vulnerable to enemy fire so tried putting it there. Not good so back it went on his head and he came back to our trenches moving backwards all the way. But we are losing men.

I am your ever loving son,

Walter

May

Dear Mother,

We're now back at the rest billets at Agnez-Les-Duisans after the unpleasant business of being in the trenches for seventeen days without a break. No opportunity even to change our clothes and wash. We shared the trenches with a quantity of verminous insects which gave us a great deal of discomfort. We were all scratching. Horrid.

We're a Battalion in support just now which is far from having a rest worse luck. Every night strong parties are called upon to do work on the front line like tunnelling. Mainly men who were miners back home do this because they are used to it. Every bit of chalk they bring out has to be disposed of where it can't be seen so it doesn't give the game away. We know the Germans are tunnelling underneath us so every few minutes we stop and listen for them tapping. It's weird. They're doing the same too. It's terribly dangerous and there are explosions and the casualties are high.

Keep those letters coming from home they cheer us up no end. And parcels of fruit cake.

Walter

P S What's this about Sidney getting married?

25th May

Dear Mother,

I'm still here in case you wondered. It's no secret, there was a disastrous raid the other night. Badly handled and many casualties but we'll do better next time.

Walter

Sunday 4th June

Dearest Mother,

What a beautiful day it is today. The sun is shining out of a clear blue sky. The larks are singing. Yet we're actually on the front line. It's hard to believe there is a war on.

God's in his heaven,
All's right with the world.

I wish it were true. The post is going soon but there is just time to tell you I often think of my family at home and wish I could be back with you. Maybe before long I shall be. Good luck to Sidney and his Minnie. Good wishes to them for a long and happy marriage.

Your ever loving son.

Walter

✱✱✱✱✱✱✱✱✱✱

That was Walter's last letter to his mother. When it arrived we were buoyed up because we'd heard there had been more heavy action on the front line but this seemed to hold out hope that he wasn't affected by it. At four o'clock on that beautiful Sunday afternoon and again in the evening the enemy guns had opened up with disastrous results and much loss of life. One of those lives was our dear Walter who was only twenty years old. I heard the scream and then silence and rushed round next door. Whatever had happened? Susannah had fainted almost on the doorstep but there in her hand was the reason. I didn't need to read the letter for it was almost identical to the one I had received telling me that Harry had been killed. I sat on the floor and cradled her head as she came round.

"My poor dear," I said. "My poor, poor dear."

"Mam, tell me it's not true." She beseeched me.

We wept together. Oh the horror, a second death in our family in this terrible war.

I helped Susannah up and she went to her bed where I could hear her moaning and crying out, "No, no, not my

Walter!"

I sat downstairs and waited for Hetty to come back from school. When she came through the door she saw my red eyes and said, "Grandma, whatever has happened?"

So I told her and we held each other and wept together before she went up to her mother. As Sidney and George came in they were told as well. While George went up to try to comfort Susannah, Sidney went round to tell Florry. The curtains were closed in the front parlour and soon the whole road knew that there had been another death in the Voyce family. Thomas and Annie came round, "Mam, that's two of our three gone. I'm so afraid for my Charley," Annie said while Thomas looked very grim.

Unlike my Harry there was a grave for Walter. Certainly Susannah was never able to visit it and I don't know if anyone else in the family managed to go to the cemetery at Faubourg d'Amiens in Arras to see it after the war. I was far too old to make the journey. There were yet more tears when Susannah saw the Midsummer edition of 'The Bridge' where Walter's death was announced among those of other old boys of the school. He had been *'a clever boy and a popular member of the football team'* it said.

"What a waste of those young lives," she said and we all agreed with her.

Susannah's health seriously declined after Walter's death. The doctor said she had Bright's disease but I knew and so did George that Walter's death had broken her heart. She didn't go to Sidney's wedding later that summer. Mostly she took to her bed but sometimes would have a chair and sit in the garden. When Sidney and Minnie's son was born the following April there was only one name that they could have chosen. The baby was baptised with Walter's name in memory of him. I think Susannah was touched by that gesture but by now she was a bedridden invalid.

26. Walter's grave at Faubourg d'Amiens, Arras, Northern France
Photo: Richard Voice

Florry gave up her job and came home to look after the household and we were all very bowed down by our grief and by Susannah's illness. The summer ended and we moved into the autumn. The angel of death had not yet finished with us. In October Thomas and Annie came round to say they had received the letter too. Charles Thomas had been killed on 12th October in Flanders.

"There, that's it," said Thomas bitterly, "we've given our brother and sons. Our coffers are empty. We can do no more."

When Susannah heard the news, as she lay in her bed, the tears welled again from her eyes, "Annie, my dear, we have nothing else to give."

27. Walter's next of kin Memorial Plaque 'Dead Man's Penny'

From that day her decline was rapid and exactly a month after Charles Thomas' death she too died. Although Doctor Sims said she died of Bright's disease and heart failure I think the real cause of her death was the terrible shock of what happened to Walter and to the other two soldiers in our family.

So there we were in the winter of 1917. The war dragged on bringing heartbreak to the families who had lost their dear ones, but nearer to home, in fact next door, there was Hetty, an orphan at thirteen. Dear dependable Florry as usual kept the boat afloat. She was now twenty-three and whatever she might have preferred to be doing she stayed at home and kept house for the two of them.

The war ended in November 1918. Maybe there was joy in some households as their loved ones returned safely, but we could only partially share that joy.

On November 11th 1919 the whole country marked Armistice Day remembering the war that had finished a year ago. Church bells were rung and at exactly eleven o'clock everything went silent for two minutes. The churches were full of people remembering the fallen. Thomas and Annie went into town and stood in Victoria Square. Afterwards, with tears streaming down her face, Annie told me, "Mam the traffic stopped, the cars and drays stopped and everyone stood still wherever they were. Men took off their hats and bowed their heads, an old soldier stood to attention and women were weeping. Birmingham has not forgotten its boys who gave their lives."

The worldwide influenza pandemic of 1918-1920 killed more people than those killed in the war, so although it was a time of joy that the war had ended it was also a time of great suffering. It may well have been a contributory factor in Sidney's death. His weak chest had stopped him going out to the trenches but he was not spared after all. He died in December 1920 just as Minnie had given birth to their daughter. In the midst of this further sadness I could only be thankful that Susannah had not lived to see the death of another son. After Susannah had died George moved out and left Florry and Hetty in the home that had been theirs for all of their lives.

One day they came round to see me with a wooden box they had found under Susannah's bed.

"Grandma, look what we have found. We had a peep inside and it seems to have old things in it so perhaps you can tell us more about them". They put the box on my table and Hetty opened the lid. Inside there were rolls of paper and some photographs. Underneath them all was something carefully wrapped up in tissue paper. Florry lifted it out and put it in front of me. I slowly pulled the paper away and there we could see some pressed flowers and a carefully folded but somewhat faded, blue ribbon.

"This is amazing," I told them, "I remember this. It's part of your mother's wedding bouquet from 1890. Charley was allowed to take some gardenias out of his employer's glass house and Alice put some lilies of the valley with them and tied them with this blue ribbon to make a bouquet. I remember this as clearly as if it was yesterday. Susannah put them in a vase of water before she and Evan went to Weston-super-Mare for their honeymoon and when they came back a week later she took some of the flowers and pressed them and when they were dry she placed them in this box. And now you have found them after all these years. Well just fancy that. The rediscovery of the flowers in her bouquet."

"How romantic," Hetty sighed.

"So what are the other things in here?" Florry asked.

"Here are some photographs; Florry, here you are with your brothers and parents. And Hetty, here's one of you as a baby, sitting on your mother's knee. Look how ill your Pa looks. He died a few weeks later. And here is one taken on their wedding day just over thirty years ago. Look, there's me and my Charley. Doesn't your Pa look handsome?" Hetty peered over my shoulder,

"There's Grandma Mary with Grandpa William. He looks a bit…."

"Don't say it, Hetty," Florry put in. "It's unkind to speak disrespectfully of the dead."

We started to unroll the pieces of paper and discovered that they were all the family birth, marriage and death certificates. "Which is the oldest one?" Florry asked.

We had a good look at them and found that the oldest was Ann Saint's death certificate from 1840.

"Look." Said Florry, "It says she was eighty years old when she died in Hereford and that she was the widow of William Saint a shoemaker. I remember my other grandma, mother's mother, talking about him and Ann and how they came from America. They must have been born in about 1760. That's a very long time ago isn't it?"

"And here's another death certificate for his son Thomas who died of consumption in Hereford Workhouse." I said.

"And here's one for his wife Susannah who died in childbirth. So Grandma Mary and three of her sisters were brought up in Hereford Workhouse." Hetty said.

"Yes," I said quietly, "She told me about that but she was ashamed of it and didn't like to talk about it as there was such a stigma attached to having been in the workhouse. Of course there still is and destitute people are terrified of having to go there. Anyway later she married your grandfather William and had a terrible time with him"

"So she had a very hard life then," Florry added.

"Yes she did," I added, "but we have too these last years."

"But we go on and manage the best we can," Florry put in on a more cheerful note.

Hetty stood up and stretched her young limbs,

"It's all over now," she said, "the 1920s are here and we're going to have fun, fun, fun! Most women have the vote, skirts are getting short, we're cutting our long hair into a bob and we're dancing the Charleston and having a good time."

"Well before you dance back next door," I added, "just think how important the contents of this box are as a record for the future. I see you haven't put Walter's next of kin Memorial Plaque into it yet. Do so, because that's going to be another piece of history. And while you're about it have a look among your mother's things for the locket she wore round her neck that had the picture of Walter in uniform in it. That should go in here as well. We don't realise that what is still almost the present for us is the history of the future."

As we moved further into the 1920s Florry and Hetty did have some fun. Dancing, moving pictures, motor cars; and above all there was freedom from the worry that had dominated recent years. Alice remarried and had another baby, a sweet little thing. Florry and Hetty still live next door and are very attentive to me, their old Welsh Grandma. They are all very dear to me as are the memories of those who have passed on.

But the years move on and I am very old now and not being one to mince matters I know that I am dying of cancer. These are my last painful days and I have taken to my bed. The nearer I get to meet my Maker the further back I go into my past. I think of my dear Charley who has gone before me, I think of my childhood at my father's mill in Kerry, of my dear mother. I think of the times she took me back to her childhood home on the Long Mynd and through the haze I can just remember her mother Ann, the wizened old lady who sat in the rocking chair in the corner of the farmhouse kitchen.

But what is this? The sky is brightening and she is not old anymore. She is a young woman and she is holding her hand out to me.

"Come with me Sarah," she says.

I hold out my hand and our fingertips touch.

"Come," she says again.

My pain is gone and I feel happy and full of life. I'm so light that I'm floating; I'm rising up. We're going up the verdant slopes of the Long Mynd with the old Drovers

Track below us but I'm not out of breath.

"Come," she says again.

I grasp her warm hand in mine and I look back.

In the haze far below me, as if in another world, I can see Alice, Florry and Hetty bending over a bed looking at a small lifeless form. They are crying.

"Don't cry my dears," I call out to them but I don't think they can hear me.

"Come," Ann says for the last time and I don't look back any more. I look forward to where she is taking me. Up here the air is pure and the larks rise singing into the cloudless sky. In the blue distance are the mountains of Wales. I have found peace.

****

It was Alice who registered her mother's death and yet again the family gathered for a funeral. It was a sombre affair as no one there could fail to realise that Sarah's sons Evan and Harry who should have still been alive had predeceased her, and her grandsons Charles Thomas, Walter and Sidney had also had their young lives cut short. Florry and Hetty felt particularly bereft as their parents and both brothers were gone.

But time moves on and two years later, in 1926 Hetty married Josiah and the next year their daughter was born. Sadly it wasn't only Susannah's marriage that was cut short by her husband's illness and death, for the same fate befell

Hetty's husband. He died of cancer in 1938 leaving their daughter fatherless at eleven years old.

Hetty was my mother and I feel great sympathy for her. The year after she was widowed the Second World War broke out. Lacking the comfort and support of her husband she was lonely and vulnerable. Memories were still fresh of the tragedies of the First World War. She was probably keeping up the insurance payments that Josiah had started. Maybe she had already benefitted from them herself or maybe she had started them again should anything happen to her during this war. Be that as it may the insurance man called weekly to collect the payments. He became attracted to the pretty young widow and she to him. Here was the male presence she craved, here was a sympathetic ear and here were warm arms that would wrap around her. Forgetting his wife and son at home he and Hetty began a passionate affair.

And then it all went wrong, for Hetty found that she was expecting his baby. As far as they were concerned an illegitimate baby was a disaster and my entrance into the world was kept secret from almost everyone. I do not know if my father's wife ever knew about this baby but certainly there was no question of him leaving her and marrying Hetty. She went to Worcester to stay with friends and my father paid for the birth to take place in a nursing home there. I found out many years later that it was there that my half-sister had held me when I was a few hours old.

Subsequently I was taken back to the family home in Birmingham but it was very difficult to keep the presence of a baby in the house a secret from the neighbours so the decision was taken that I should be adopted. My half-sister told me that from the moment I was take away to be adopted she and Hetty never again mentioned the baby that had been born. It was as if it had not happened. That was how things were in those days; what was behind you was over and done with, you had to get on with life. Poor Hetty, so many tragedies in her life and now a baby, lost and never ever mentioned again. However when the war had ended she had happier times and became a nursery school teacher.

28. Hetty

And, just in case you want to know, everything went well for me. I had a happy childhood in my adoptive home, became a teacher, have a loving marriage and have sons and grandchildren.

My half-sister also had a long and loving marriage and with her husband built up a very successful business.

The Flowers in my Bouquet is about my ancestors gathered together, like flowers in a bouquet. Writing and researching the material for this book has enabled me to get to know them and has drawn me very close to their lives and the often hard times in which they lived. As I have researched their lives I have come to realise how very different the times in which they lived are from our own.

Before the days of birth control women were worn down by repeated childbirth; death in childbirth was much more likely to happen than it is today. The medical advances which have benefitted subsequent generations were not available to them. To lose a child before the age of five from diseases treatable today was commonplace. We have the advantage of immunisation for common childhood diseases and antibiotics to help with recovery from ailments.

Among my ancestors there were several deaths from TB. Since the introduction of antibiotics after the Second World War and the general improvement in living conditions, that is a very rare occurrence as is TB itself in the western world. We have the benefit of modern sanitation with clean water and efficient sewerage systems. But within living memory we can look back on homes without bathrooms, that had toilets 'down the yard' or even privies shared by others in a courtyard.

The Voice/Voyce family, like many others in this country and elsewhere suffered tragically from the effects of war. No doubt there will always be wars but for them the Great War and the influenza pandemic that followed it were terrible times to live through.

I began this story by wondering 'Who do I think I am?'

Now I know the answer.

Photos taken in later life of family members mentioned in the book

29. **Matilda Jane Voyce**
1863-1953

30. Richard Rhodes Briggs
1868-1941

31. William Voyce Briggs
1904-1983

32. Mary Goode, née Hall, 1875-1964,
With her Granddaughter and Great Granddaughter
Photo courtesy of William Clark

33. Thomas Voice and Family
Photo courtesy of Richard Voice

34. Hetty, 1904-1981 and Florry, 1894-1963

Chapter Notes

In writing this book I have made extensive use of birth, marriage and death records, both those found online and in certificates obtained from the General Register Office.

Ancestry.co.uk and the Internet have been used extensively.

I have also consulted The British Newspaper Archives.

Chapter 2

On the Drovers' Trail

Thomas Howells: married Jane Davies on October 1st 1764 at the church of St Michael and All Angels, Lydbury North, near Bishops Castle, Shropshire.

Thomas and Jane Howells: the births and baptisms of Thomas and Jane Howells' children and of **Ann's** two children are found in the church records for **Myndtown Church, Shropshire**.

Sarah Howells and Evan Watkin's marriage is recorded in the records of Kerry Church as is Sarah Watkin's baptism on 7th February 1836.

The Watkin family: information about the Watkin family is obtained from census records and birth, marriage and death records from 1837 onwards.

Chapter 3

The Journey Back

William Saint: in the White House in Washington there is a record of a William Saint born in Williamsburg in 1759 who was a boot and scabbard maker for a foot regiment. There is no proof that it is the same William Saint.

Triangle of Trade: the sailing ship that William and Ann Saint would have travelled on would have been part of the Triangle of Trade that took cloth, trinkets and ammunition from England to Africa where these commodities were bartered for slaves. The next leg of the journey was called The Middle Passage when slaves were crammed into the hold of the ship which, relying on the Trade Winds, made the journey to the Caribbean or New England. Those slaves that survived the journey were sold to work on sugar, cotton or tobacco plantations. The third leg of the journey was back to England using the winds associated with the Gulf Stream where those commodities were sold. The whole process could take a year. This trade lasted from the 16th to the mid-19th century.

The Slave Trade Act: in 1807 the United Kingdom Government passed The Slave Trade Act abolishing the trading of slaves in the British Empire. In 1833 an Act was passed abolishing slavery in most of the British Empire.

The Loyalists who returned later like William and Ann were called **Late Loyalists** and some of them received pensions from the Government but although a search has been made there was no record of William Saint being among them.

Margaret Saint: church records for St Peters, Hereford show that Margaret Saint married Job Blick on 11th Dec 1811. They moved to Kidderminster where Job Blick was a carpet weaver. The 1851 census in Kidderminster records that Margaret Blick was born in America in about 1791.

The sale of the land in 1806 that William Saint owned with James Gore and Thomas Williams is recorded in The Hereford Times.

Pigot's 1830 Directory for Hereford: information regarding James Saint was obtained from censuses and from Pigot's 1830 Directory for Hereford.

St Owen's graveyard where, according to the national Burial Records, William was buried in 1823, has succumbed to development in Hereford.

St Owen's Church was demolished during the Civil War as it was felt that its position close to the exterior of the city walls might aid the parliamentary forces.

St Owen's Gate was demolished in 1782.

Chapter Four

The Hereford Years

'Grogram' gowns worn by the female inmates were made

of a coarse fabric of silk or mohair and wool or a mixture of these often stiffened with gum.

Linsey-Woolsey was a fabric with a linen, or sometimes cotton, warp and a wool weft. Sometimes its name is linked with the village of Lindsey in Suffolk or simply derived from 'Lin' an old name for flax.

William Saint, the policeman, is mentioned in the Hereford Times.

The Hereford Times was also the source of the Inquest report on **Catherine Saint's** death and the report of **Jane's trial**.

"I'm going to warn you Susannah Morgan that though the pitcher might go often to the well it was sure to be broken at last and yours is cracked." "Aye it is," she said, "and it was you who cracked it".

Meaning obscure; these were the actual words spoken at the trial as reported by The Hereford Times. Obviously meant derogatively.

Moving On

William Hall's Police record gives a detailed list of his failings as a policeman in Birmingham.

Chapter Five

Starting Out

Carrs Lane Congregational Church that Susannah attended with Florence was demolished at the end of the 1960s and replaced with a modern church centre which opened in 1970.

A Royal Visit

Christ Church at the top of New Street was demolished in 1899.

Chapter 6

Sarah from Wales

Railways: by the 1850's the spread of the railways enabled people to move around more easily than they had done previously.

Weather statistics show that the summer of 1860 was one of the wettest on record.

Castle Bromwich: census records for 1861 have provided the details about Castle Bromwich.

Alick and Betty Voice, variously spelt **Vice, Voyce or Vyse,** were tenants of Lord Bradford whose estate records are in the Staffordshire Record office.

Mr John Bateman the architect did live at Hawkeshead House in Castle Bromwich and Charles Voice's cottage was very close to that but it is pure conjecture on my part that he employed Charles.

Almost all of **Charles and Sarah Voice's** children spelt their surname as Voice, but when Evan Charles Voice married, the spelling he used for his surname and thereafter for himself and his children was **Voyce** apart from the 1901 census. Also he signed his marriage certificate as Charles Evan Voyce. Thus we have two brothers **Thomas Voice** and **Evan Charles Voyce** spelling their surnames differently and two cousins, **Charles Thomas Voice** on the Tyne Cot memorial and **Walter Charles Voyce** on the grave in the Faubourg d'Amiens cemetery in Arras.

Harold Edward Voyce (1881-1914) It had been a puzzle that I could not find his birth registration, nor find him on a census, until 1901. Yet there at Wellington Road on the 1891 census was Edward Harold Benbow who had the same date of birth as Harold Voyce, 25th November 1881. It was only when I obtained Edward Benbow's birth certificate and found that he was the illegitimate son of Jessie Benbow, daughter of Sarah's sister Mary, that I realised he and Harold were the same person and that Sarah and Charles Voice had adopted him.

Matilda Jane Voice used the Voyce spelling on the 1891 census when she was working in Cheshire and on her marriage certificate.

Chapter 7

Married Life 1890-1904

Ethel Voyce lived for seventeen months and died of hydrocephalus on 2nd January 1894.

Bingley Hall in Birmingham was the first purpose built exhibition hall in Great Britain. It was built in 1850 and burnt down in 1984.

Winston Churchill (1874-1965) was an officer in the British Army, a historian, a writer and an artist. He was a British politician who was Prime Minister of the United Kingdom from 1940 to 1945 and from 1951 to 1955. He is widely regarded as one of the greatest wartime leaders of the 20th century.

Robert Baden–Powell, Lord Baden-Powell (1857-1941) was a lieutenant-general in the British Army, writer, founder of the Scout Movement and first Chief Scout of The Boy Scout Association.

Chapter 8

Widowhood 1904-1914

Alice Dolan, née Voice, remarried in the summer of 1907 becoming Alice Jones.

Henry Hurst Jan 4th 1909 Henry Hurst's name was on Harry and Eleanor's marriage certificate as a witness to the marriage.

Thomas and Annie's son Sidney Howard born in 1905 was baptized with Winifred, Henry and Horace in May 1909 at All Saints Hockley.

Charles Thomas Voice resigned from the railways in 1910 and became a barman.
In Oct 1914 at the age of twenty-one he married Charlotte Titley.

In the 1911 census:

Sidney Voyce was a gardener living at home aged 20.
Florry Voyce was a live-in servant in Aston.
Walter Voyce, aged 15, was at school.
Hetty Voyce, aged 7, was at school
Thomas Voice was a postman.
Charles Thomas Voice was a barman.
John Clarence Voice was a jewellers' machinist.
Harold Voice was an assistant carter.

Chapter 9

The Great War and Beyond, 1914-1924

Eleanor Voyce lived in widowhood until her death in 1971 when she was eighty-nine.

The War Diary of the 15th Battalion of the Royal Warwickshire Regiment provided much useful material charting Walter's active service, including the places he must have marched through and been stationed at.

Charlotte Voice: after three years as a widow, Charlotte Voice née Titley married Hubert Vale in 1920. In 1951 her son Charles William Voice, with his wife Ellen and three children, emigrated to Sydney, Australia where he died in 1978.

The WW1 transcription, online, of the War Diary of acting Cpl James Strangeway of the 2nd Battalion Rifle Brigade, whilst not giving specific information about Charles Thomas Voice who was in the 7th Battalion, gives some interesting background information.

Lord Kitchener drowned at sea on 5th June 1916, the day after Walter was killed.

In Flanders Fields

In Flanders fields the poppies blow
Between the crosses, row on row
That mark our place; and in the sky
The larks, still bravely singing, fly
Scarce heard amid the guns below.

This poem written in 1915 by Canadian physician Lieutenant Colonel John McCrae inspired the wearing of poppies on November 11th from 1920 onwards.

Family Trees

For ease of viewing the family trees can also be accessed on the author's website

www.susiewilliams.coffeecup.com

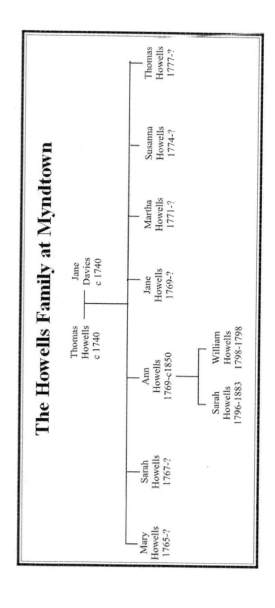

The Howells Family at Myndtown

Thomas Howells c 1740 — Jane Davies c 1740

Mary Howells 1765-?

Sarah Howells 1767-?

Ann Howells 1769-c1850
- Sarah Howells 1796-1883
- William Howells 1798-1798

Jane Howells 1769-?

Martha Howells 1771-?

Susanna Howells 1774-?

Thomas Howells 1777-?

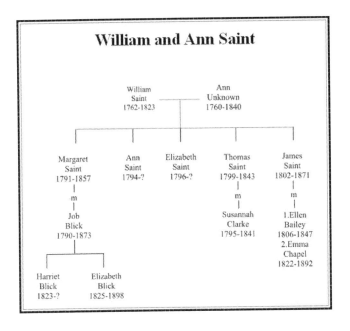

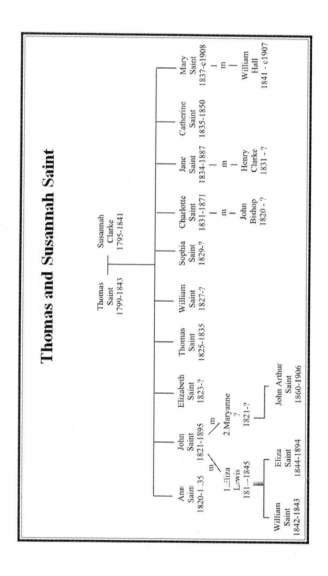

Thomas and Susannah Saint

Thomas Saint 1790-1843

Susannah Clarke 1795-1841

- John Saint 1820-1895
  - m 1.Eliza Lewis 181?-1845
    - William Saint 1842-1843
    - Eliza Saint 1844-1894
  - m 2.Maryanne ? 1821-?
    - John Arthur Saint 1860-1906
- Ann Saint 1820-1835
- Elizabeth Saint 1823-?
- Thomas Saint 1825-1835
- William Saint 1827-?
- Sophia Saint 1829-?
- Charlotte Saint 1831-1871
  - m John Bishop 1820-?
- Jane Saint 1834-1887
  - m Henry Clarke 1831-?
- Catherine Saint 1835-1850
- Mary Saint 1837-c1908
  - m William Hall 1841-c1907

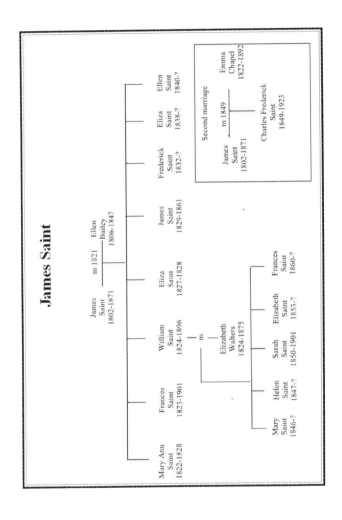

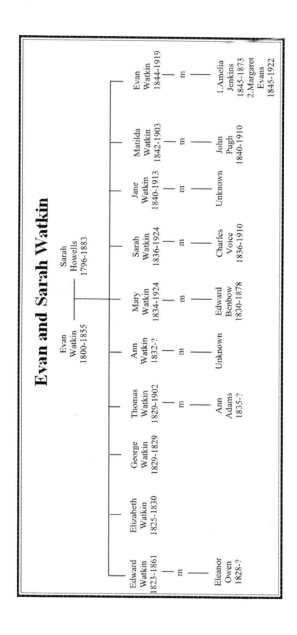

Evan and Sarah Watkin

Evan Watkin 1800-1855 — Sarah Howells 1796-1883

Edward Watkin 1823-1861	Elizabeth Watkin 1825-1830	George Watkin 1829-1829	Thomas Watkin 1829-1902	Ann Watkin 1832-?	Mary Watkin 1834-1924	Sarah Watkin 1836-1924	Jane Watkin 1840-1913	Matilda Watkin 1842-1903	Evan Watkin 1844-1919
m			m	m	m	m	m	m	m
Eleanor Owen 1828-?			Ann Adams 1835-?	Unknown	Edward Benbow 1830-1878	Charles Voice 1836-1910	Unknown	John Pugh 1840-1910	1.Amelia Jenkins 1845-1873 2.Margaret Evans 1845-1922

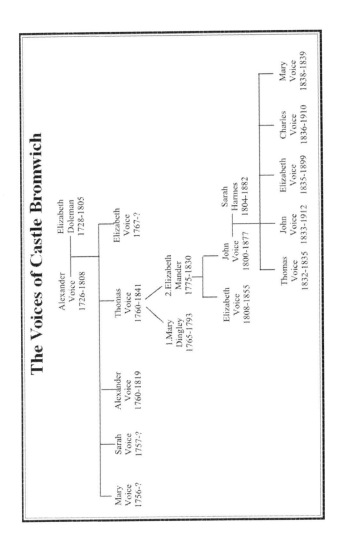

The Voices of Castle Bromwich

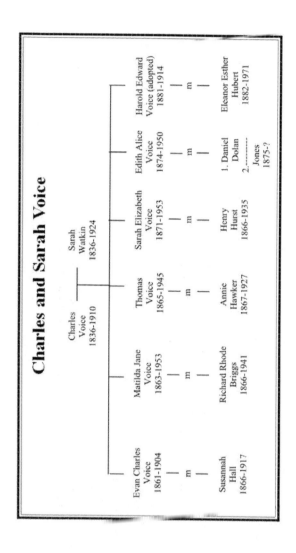

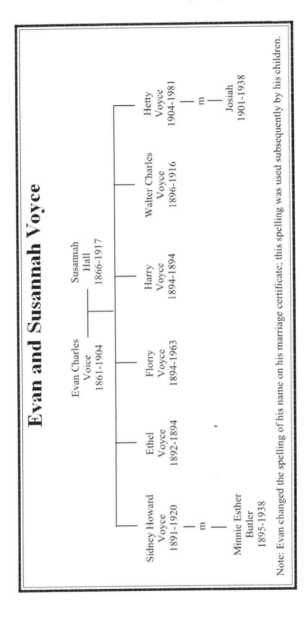

Evan and Susannah Voyce

Evan Charles Voice 1861-1904 — Susannah Hall 1866-1917

Sidney Howard Voyce 1891-1920 — m — Minnie Esther Butler 1895-1938

Ethel Voyce 1892-1894

Florry Voyce 1894-1963

Harry Voyce 1894-1894

Walter Charles Voyce 1896-1916

Hetty Voyce 1904-1981 — m — Josiah 1901-1938

Note: Evan changed the spelling of his name on his marriage certificate; this spelling was used subsequently by his children.

Susie Williams

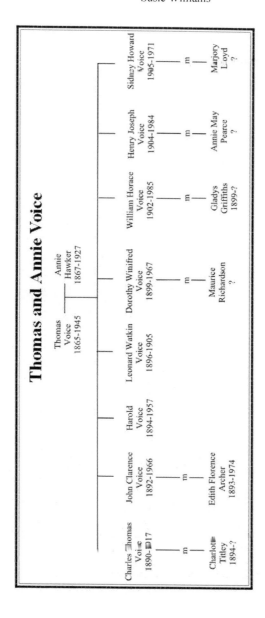

322

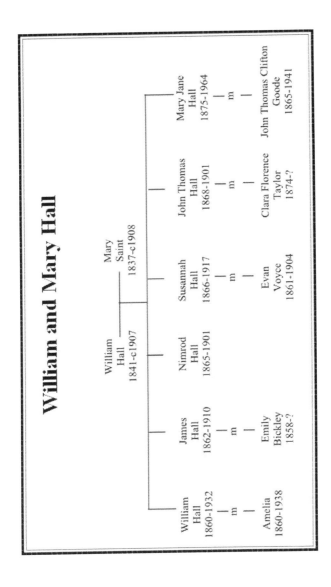

William and Mary Hall

William Hall
1841-c1907

Mary Saint
1837-c1908

William Hall
1860-1932
m
Amelia
1860-1938

James Hall
1862-1910
m
Emily Bickley
1858-?

Nimrod Hall
1865-1901

Susannah Hall
1866-1917
m
Evan Voyce
1861-1904

John Thomas Hall
1868-1901
m
Clara Florence Taylor
1874-?

Mary Jane Hall
1875-1964
m
John Thomas Clifton Goode
1865-1941

Susie Williams

Website www.susiewilliams.coffeecup.com

e-mail susiewilliams842@gmail.com

Back cover photo

St John the Baptist, Myndtown